Regulating the Metaverse

The metaverse seems to be on everybody's lips – and yet, very few people can actually explain what it means or why it is important. This book aims to fill the gap from an interdisciplinary perspective informed by law and media and communications studies. Going beyond the optimism emanating from technology companies and venture capitalists, the authors critically evaluate the antecedents and the building blocks of the metaverse, the design and regulatory challenges that need to be solved, and commercial opportunities that are yet to be fully realised. While the metaverse is poised to open new possibilities and perspectives, it will also be a dangerous place – one ripe with threats ranging from disinformation to intellectual property theft to sexual harassment. Hence, the book offers a useful guide to the legal and political governance issues ahead while also contextualising them within the broader domain of governance and regulation of digital technologies.

Ignas Kalpokas is Associate Professor in the Department of Public Communication, Vytautas Magnus University, Kaunus, Lithuania, where he also heads the MA programme Future Media and Journalism. His research focuses on the social and political impact of digital technologies, fake news and information warfare, and media theory. Ignas's teaching stretches across the domains of journalism and media studies, disinformation and propaganda studies, and geopolitics of the internet. He is the author of *Creativity and Limitation in Political Communities: Spinoza, Schmitt, and Ordering* (Routledge, 2018), *A Political Theory of Post-Truth* (Palgrave Macmillan, 2019), *Algorithmic Governance: Politics and Law in the Post-Human Era* (Palgrave Macmillan, 2019), and *Malleable, Digital, and Posthuman: A Permanently Beta Life* (Emerald, 2021), and co-author of *Deepfakes: A Realistic Assessment of Potentials, Risks, and Policy Regulation* (Springer, 2022).

Julija Kalpokienė is a qualified Lithuanian attorney specialising in commercial law and dispute resolution with a particular interest in intellectual property, data protection, and IT law. She is a PhD candidate at Vytautas Magnus University, Kaunus, Lithuania, where she is a Junior Research Fellow, teaches Technology Law, and is course leader for An Interdisciplinary Introduction to AI. Julija also has experience in internet governance and policy work. Her research focuses on internet regulation, cybercrime, technology regulation, with a particular focus on AI and creativity, and more generally intellectual property and privacy law. Julija is also an active member of the Lithuanian Young Bar Association where she is Vice-Chair of the Kaunas Chapter and a member of the Information Committee. She is co-author of *Deepfakes: A Realistic Assessment of Potentials, Risks, and Policy Regulation* (Springer, 2022).

Law of Emerging Technologies Series

Routledge Research in the Law of Emerging Technologies

Biometrics, Surveillance and the Law
Societies of Restricted Access, Discipline and Control
Sara M. Smyth

Artificial Intelligence, Healthcare, and the Law
Regulating Automation in Personal Care
Eduard Fosch-Villaronga

Health Data Privacy under the GDPR
Big Data Challenges and Regulatory Responses
Edited by Maria Tzanou

Regulating Artificial Intelligence
Binary Ethics and the Law
Dominika Ewa Harasimiuk and Tomasz Braun

Cryptocurrencies and Regulatory Challenge
Allan C. Hutchinson

Regulating Artificial Intelligence in Industry
Edited by Damian M. Bielicki

The Law of Global Digitality
Edited by Matthias C. Kettemann, Alexander Peukert and Indra Spiecker gen. Döhmann

Internet of Things and the Law
Legal Strategies for Consumer-Centric Smart Technologies
Guido Noto La Diega

Regulating the Metaverse
A Critical Assessment
Ignas Kalpokas and Julija Kalpokienė

For more information about this series, please visit: https://www.routledge.com/Routledge-Research-in-the-Law-of-Emerging-Technologies/book-series/LAWTECHNOLOGY

Regulating the Metaverse

A Critical Assessment

Ignas Kalpokas and Julija Kalpokienė

Routledge
Taylor & Francis Group
LONDON AND NEW YORK

First published 2023
by Routledge
4 Park Square, Milton Park, Abingdon, Oxon OX14 4RN

and by Routledge
605 Third Avenue, New York, NY 10158

Routledge is an imprint of the Taylor & Francis Group, an informa business

British Library Cataloguing-in-Publication Data

A catalogue record for this book is available from the British Library

ISBN: 978-1-032-41019-7 (hbk)
ISBN: 978-1-032-41020-3 (pbk)
ISBN: 978-1-003-35586-1 (ebk)

DOI: 10.4324/9781003355861

Typeset in Times New Roman
by Deanta Global Publishing Services, Chennai, India

Contents

1 Introduction

The aim of this book is to examine the many shades of grey within ongoing trends and practices, business endeavours, regulatory attempts, and future projections to paint a realistic picture of the metaverse. In doing so, it ultimately transpires that, despite the innovations involved, the metaverse remains firmly rooted in (mostly) the same human habits and traits as are current technologies and will likely continue many of the same business practices and corporate models that characterise the current platform ecosystem (often deepening them even further). No doubt, the metaverse is promising, there are opportunities for individuals and businesses, and it very likely represents the future. However, it also deserves a look from outside the hype bubble. This is exactly what this book strives to achieve.

While there is only limited coherence in existing definitions of the metaverse, some broad themes can be identified. According to Balis (2022), 'the metaverse includes any digital experience on the internet that is persistent, immersive, three-dimensional (3D), and virtual'. There is also at least some consensus over the forthcoming use of the metaverse: that, in one way or another, it would become 'a shared virtual space where users lead varied lives in avatar form: shopping, working and socialising in a fantasy world' (Faber 2022; see also Koss 2020; Ball 2022). For others, it is 'a future iteration of the internet, made up of persistent, shared, 3D virtual spaces linked into a perceived virtual universe' (Hackl 2020). Hence, the metaverse would constitute a virtual world that would compete with, or perhaps replace, the physical world in terms of its importance for personal, social, economic, and political life. Still, just like the physical world, despite being one in an overarching sense, contains a vast diversity of natural and human-made partitions, its virtual counterpart may well be to some extent interoperable but, nevertheless, not unitary, leaving room for numerous business models to coexist.

Moreover, while internet access is currently mostly synonymous with smartphones and computers, VR headsets and, subsequently, glasses or

DOI: 10.4324/9781003355861-1

other less obtrusive access devices will be the next iteration of connectivity technology, supplemented with 'haptic devices that allow users to actually "feel" virtual objects', enabling a simulation of physical-world experiences (Wiederhold 2022: 1). If this vision is brought to fruition, the metaverse would be bound to become 'the gateway to most digital experiences, a key component of all physical ones, and the next great labor platform' (Ball 2020), meaning that the physical world itself will no longer be the default experience. Thus, the metaverse would become 'a shared interface [...] to connect virtual experiences with the augmented reality-enhanced physical world' (Threekit n.d.). Clearly, then, the commercial interest in the metaverse is easy to understand.

While immersion in digital life has been possible for a while, prior to the COVID-19 pandemic it had been relatively niche, sometimes even frowned upon or seen as a social dysfunction, particularly in its more extreme forms that lead to self-seclusion (see e.g. Rooksby, McLeod and Fururashi 2020). Meanwhile, the pandemic has normalised digital-first life, bringing about 'a revalorization of digital interactions as valuable and meaningful', simultaneously accelerating the adoption of technological affordances even by those who would otherwise have lagged behind (Mantegna 2021). Indeed, the ability to socialise and attend events without leaving one's home suddenly became much more attractive than ever before (Snider 2021). After all, for many, particularly younger, users, the ever-deepening digital (and virtual) shift does not even represent that much of a cultural break or change in everyday practices, because today's children and youth are already growing up in a proto-metaverse online space (Clark 2021), from social media to gaming and esports. If the metaverse was to materialise, it would, therefore, be not revolutionary but simply a further step within a process of largely evolutionary change. Even more fundamentally, it could be argued that the intertwining between humans and technology is already so close that the distinction between 'conventional' and virtual reality is problematic even now (Chan 2022: 129–130). Hence, any talk about radical novelty and unprecedentedness of the metaverse should be taken with a pinch of salt. Simultaneously, though, the relative 'normality' of the metaverse should, at least in theory, contribute to its uptake among users as the cost of switching would be lower than for something that completely breaks with the past.

Consistently, 'as computers have become more capable, the experiences that they generate have become richer', from plain text to pictures to videos to virtual experiences; the same can be said of games and other increasingly sophisticated digital environments (*The Economist* 2021). Nevertheless, the realism of the metaverse (or lack thereof) does not seem to be a completely settled matter either: while some would expect full-scale replication of people and goods (Murphy 2022), fantasy worlds by themselves constitute part of the attraction. It is also more than likely that different platforms that will together constitute the metaverse will embrace different degrees of realism, as is already present in today's proto-metaverse platforms (compare e.g. Meta's Horizon Worlds with *Fortnite* or with *Roblox*). What matters, however, is that the metaverse becomes an interface for content and experiences. As an interface, the metaverse is perhaps best conceivable in terms of utilisation of both hardware and software 'to enable interaction with a simulated, three-dimensional environment, in real time' (Zhou, Leenders and Cong 2018: 57). This, however, also constitutes one of the most significant challenges in bringing about a truly immersive metaverse – the hardware necessary for real-time rendering of content would have to significantly increase in power while becoming more lightweight and comfortable to wear; likewise, the storage requirements associated with the persistence of virtual worlds would be immense (Ball 2022: 36–37, 46).

While earlier examples, such as *Second Life*, were primarily concerned with creation of *alternative* realities, the key driver for the metaverse is enclosing *both* the virtual and physical worlds (Virgilio 2022). Hence, the metaverse will be a space for interaction (with both humans and AI-powered avatars) and data extraction. While the claims made by tech CEOs are often bordering on outlandish, one recurrent theme is clear – '[f]or its makers, the metaverse will be stuffed with money – in every dimension, all the way down' (Wiener 2022). Hence, it may not come as a surprise that 'the Metaverse has become the newest macro-goal for many of the world's tech giants' (Ball 2020). As such companies are always on the lookout for the 'next big thing' to capitalise on before their competitors do, 'the metaverse is exciting because it presents an opportunity for new markets, new kinds of social network, new consumer electronics and new patents' (Kelly 2021). Hence, growth opportunities are present throughout the technology stack.

It is only natural that, with the growing prominence of metaverse-related discussions, 'predictions about it have seemed mainly to reflect the desires of the corporations that are setting the terms of the conversation' (Wiener 2022). One can imagine with relative ease why, for some, the metaverse quintessentially means 'a fantasy of power and control' (Bogost 2021). A crucial appeal of the metaverse, at least for technology companies, is its ability to connect 'the rather prosaic reality of technologized consumer attention to a science-fictional dream of escape' (Bogost 2021). This combined fantasy of power, control, and escape is not unique to the metaverse but has other manifestations as well: as Zickgraf (2021) somewhat ironically observes, while other technology CEOs may invest in interplanetary travel, Mark Zuckerberg is investing in leaving the physical space altogether. Of course, such fixation on the metaverse is characteristic of more than one CEO, which only increases the complexity of this virtual world. What all of those (physical or virtual) attempts at escape have in common, however, is a sense of technological solutionism in the attempt to squeeze as much as possible (and more) of human and planetary capacities, presumably to stretch revenue beyond what is naturally possible.

Given the ground still to be covered to make the metaverse a feasible consumer option, it should come as no surprise that 'the idea is still amorphous, and a fully functioning metaverse is probably years and billions of dollars away' (Duffy 2021). Moreover, technological developments (particularly visions of a technology-enhanced future) are susceptible to hype and fantasy, existing within 'a space in which shared cultural delusions – both hopeful and fearful – can create a magic of their own independent of technical constraints, conjuring up futuristic scenarios', which are supposed to become reality if only sufficient expectation and buzz are created (Murray 2020: 13). For others, it is the lack of clarity that constitutes the defining weakness of the current debates about the metaverse: as Volpicelli (2021) puts it, 'everyone claims to be building it, but no one knows what it really will be or what it should look like'. Even so, industry insiders are struggling to contain their enthusiasm, promising that the metaverse is 'inevitable, unavoidable and, most importantly, incredibly exciting' (Holmes 2021). It is, therefore, important to strike a balance between the criticism and the hype.

According to metaverse insiders, this new assemblage of virtual worlds 'will touch every industry and profession, enlarging and/or disrupting today's leaders, and leading to countless new companies and technologies' (Takahashi 2021). One could be forgiven for thinking one has heard something like this before: such promises are repeated, almost verbatim, in relation to every next big thing, be it (in the old days) the internet, then mobile and social media, then artificial intelligence. And while much of that promise has (or will likely) come true, it is still necessary to put such bold claims into perspective, particularly with regard to the many unforeseen (or previously downplayed) effects of the aforementioned technologies that have led to, among other things, security threats and regulatory challenges. Likewise, not all of the pathways taken have proved to be equally successful (think, for example, of the dot-com bubble).

If fully realised, the metaverse is also likely to have profound offline effects, although not all such predictions seem equally credible. An argument is often made that the metaverse would lead to a diminishing importance of urban life and country of residence to participation in a high-value economy as many workers would be able to carry out their work via the metaverse (Ball 2020; Winters 2021: 17). It is important to keep in mind that even current means of connectivity have largely integrated vast populations into the digital economy on a global basis, the problem being that it is typically the low-paying, tedious jobs (such as data labelling) that get globalised. In that sense, there may be less of a levelling factor than sometimes anticipated. In terms of the more immediate lived environment, though, change can be expected: if work, social interactions, leisure, education etc. increasingly move to the metaverse, current investment in transportation and related infrastructure would turn out to have been futile. After all, the goal is for digital objects, artefacts, and experiences to have at least the same value as physical ones, bridging the boundary between the two environments (Batchelor 2021). Indeed, if physical and digital seem equally real, and the virtual version of the physical can be digitally touched and otherwise experienced through haptic technologies – all instantaneously – then travelling to a physical location might no longer be an attractive option.

The above would also mean that an even greater proportion of our lives will be dictated by rules, standards, and affordances set by unaccountable corporate actors motivated by goals other than the social good (Kelly 2021). Indeed, a key question is one of control: whether the metaverse evolves into a decentralised entity where multiple stakeholders set the standards collectively or becomes dominated by one or several key players. If past experience is a blueprint for what is to come, then the latter is the more likely outcome: we may start with a large number of competing platforms, but ultimately several will become dominant owing to their network effects (Batchelor 2021; Oi 2021; for more on network effects, see Srnicek 2017). In short, the more people join in and the more time they spend, the higher the price for refusing to join the dominant platforms (Canales 2021). With that in mind, the discourse around the metaverse seems oddly reminiscent of the early internet where the talk of openness and interoperability (even of 'independence' of cyberspace – see e.g. Barlow 1996), once prevalent, was pushed aside as soon as the profits to be made became apparent (Morse and Stein 2022).

While it is often convenient to think of the metaverse as a single entity (a viewpoint also strengthened by much of the current reporting that constantly credits one company or another as building or aiming to build *the* metaverse), it is, in fact, best conceived as a plurality. In this sense, Meta (or Epic or Microsoft or any other single company) is not building *the* metaverse, just like Facebook or Google is not *the* internet, or *Fortnite* and *Minecraft* do not, taken in isolation, constitute *the* game (for a similar argument, see also Hackl, Lueth and Di Bartolo 2022: 11). All of them are nodes within broader technological ecosystems. In that sense, no single company is building *the* metaverse, although collectively they may be. Likewise, Ball (2022: 43–44) describes the metaverse as an all-encompassing universe populated by multiple 'metagalaxies' (i.e. platforms) that are themselves composed of virtual worlds (games and experiences within platforms).

Thus, it will be up to every company or other entity to decide on 'its own access, membership, monetization rights, and formats of creative expression', leading to clear variation in both technological specifications and business strategies – as such, the metaverse is little more than an overarching concept (Balis 2022).

The above at least partly explains the variety of designs and approaches as 'every company is trying to shape the metaverse according to their strengths and strategies, each using the same world to articulate different visions' (Faber 2022). While the creation of the Metaverse Standards Forum might lead to some interoperability and, therefore, attractiveness to early adopters, just like common standards for the current Web do not mean it is borderless and not filled with walled corporate gardens in practice, there does not seem to be sufficient reason to believe that the founding members would completely overhaul their business models. Shared standards already exist in the current Web in that you can access it (and the various platforms therein) from effectively any device, but this does not contribute to actual unity online; similarly, you can use the same picture format on Facebook, Instagram, LinkedIn, and most other social media, but that still does not involve uploading a picture on one platform and having it synchronised across all your accounts on all platforms.

Instead, the way the metaverse is taking shape is as a (thus far) loose agglomeration of platforms. While platforms will be discussed in greater detail in the next chapter, suffice it to say that, with particular relevance to this discussion, a platform should be understood as 'a programmable digital architecture designed to organize interactions between users' that operates with data collection and processing at the heart of its design (van Dijck, Poell and de Waal 2018: 4). In this way, it is possible to identify certain main features of platforms that enable them to shape not merely private lives but also the organisation of entire societies: as van Dijck, Poell and de Waal (2018: 9) observe, 'a platform is fuelled by *data*, automated and organized through *algorithms* and *interfaces*, formalized through *ownership* relations driven by *business models*, and governed through *user agreements*'. Data is at the heart of such platforms, enabling both their operation *and*, simultaneously, the core product manufactured; data, however, can only be made sense of and properly used through the employment of algorithms; at the same time, users do not simply leave their data for nothing: interfaces are necessary to entice them, and make it as easy as possible, to give away their data. The metaverse, it will be shown, would be structured around data in an even more fundamental way.

Crucially, platforms also have the function of privatising entire domains of life, transforming the dynamics of such domains to suit their own business models. In this way, the governance function within societies is heavily affected as well, introducing private algorithmic governance in addition to, and sometimes in lieu of, traditional government regulation, with internal platform rules and standards becoming the new blueprint for behaviour. As will be shown in the subsequent chapters, the metaverse brings all of those issues at least one step further by intensifying datafication, leaving nothing outside the virtual interface and its algorithmic governance, deepening the proprietary modes of control and their influence on everyday life, and rendering such life subservient to the prevalent business model while any user agreements would cover a significantly broader proportion of everyday life than those of today's platforms – in fact, a metaverse platform would be, for its user, at least as much as what all other platforms of today are combined. That would, in effect, fulfil the ultimate end goal of platformisation – to become the platform for the entire life (see e.g. Vaidhyanathan 2018).

Additionally, some clarification of terminology is necessary because different authors writing on the metaverse tend to attach different connotations to the term 'platform' – or, worse, multiple meanings simultaneously. By claiming that the metaverse will continue on the platformisation path, we do not mean operating systems – already, today, platforms of the current Web operate equally well across Android and iOS, Windows and MacOS. Neither do we mean devices and their ecosystems – for example, cross-playing on Xbox and PlayStation is already a norm. Instead, we expect many, but not necessarily all, online platform companies as well as new, metaverse-native entrants to act as mostly separate clusters that become increasingly all-encompassing to the extent that one would be able to comfortably live one's entire online life within a single platform without seriously considering moving to the competition. At the end of the day, platforms acquire their importance by acting as intermediators between humans, machines, and other environmental and technological factors (Barns 2019: 9) but do so in a very specific way: while the early conception of the internet was one of openness and interaction, platforms have the effect of partitioning it into multiple corporate-owned walled gardens (Blanke and Prybus 2020: 1). With the metaverse, though, such intermediation would become particularly clear by necessitating physical gear to immerse oneself into a digitally manufactured and AI-moderated environment in which one's body movements are replicated by an avatar while, with further development of haptic technology, the avatar's 'bodily' interactions will be felt by the physical body. In that sense, the metaverse presents itself as a case of effective merger between the human and the technological.

The book opens with a consideration of the context, trends, and theoretical assumptions pertaining to the metaverse and setting a path for its emergence and further development. Subsequently, both the reasons behind the metaverse hype and its potential shortcomings are outlined, thereby aiming to provide a fair and balanced account of this virtual world of worlds. Next, the discussion moves to the metaverse economy, connecting entrepreneurial opportunities and transformations of social and personal life that together constitute new earning potential for companies and individuals while simultaneously reproducing some of the more troubling current online trends. The latter theme, although with a more pronounced emphasis on social theory, is continued into the penultimate substantial chapter of the book, presenting the changes to individual and social life brought about by the metaverse as part of a broader posthuman turn. Such changes also unavoidably bring about questions of governance and the way norms are set and enforced. Accordingly, the second part of that chapter focuses precisely on the issues of power and control of the metaverse. Finally, the last substantive chapter is dedicated to the intersection of threats and regulation while elucidating both continuity and change in the threat landscape.

Bibliography

Balis, J. (2022, January 3). How Brands Can Enter the Metaverse. *Harvard Business Review*, https://hbr.org/2022/01/how-brands-can-enter-the-metaverse.

Ball, M. (2020). The Metaverse: Where to Find It, who will Build It, and Fortnite, https://www.matthewball.vc/all/themetaverse.

Ball, M. (2022). *The Metaverse and How It will Revolutionize Everything*. New York: Liveright Publishing Corporation.

Barlow, J. P. (1996). A Declaration of the Independence of Cyberspace. Electronic Frontier Foundation, https://www.eff.org/cyberspace-independence.

Barns, S. (2019). Negotiating the Platform Pivot: From Participatory Digital Ecosystems to Infrastructures of Everyday Life. *Geography Compass*, 13(9), 1–13.

Batchelor, J. (2021, August 20). What Is the Metaverse, and Why Is It Worth so Much Money? *Games Industry*, https://www.gamesindustry.biz/articles/2021-08-20-what-is-the-metaverse-and-why-is-it-worth-so-much-money.

Blanke, T. and Pybus, J. (2020). The Material Conditions of Platforms: Monopolization Through Decentralization. *Social Media + Society*, doi: 10.1177/2056305120971632.

Bogost, I. (2021, October 28). The Metaverse Is Bad. *The Atlantic*, https://www.theatlantic.com/technology/archive/2021/10/facebook-metaverse-name-change/620449/.

Canales, C. (2021, December 4). Silicon Valley's Metaverse will Suck Reality into the Virtual World – and Ostracize those Who Are not Plugged In. *Business Insider*, https://www.businessinsider.com/metaverse-zuckerberg-facebook-virtual-world-leave-people-behind-2021-12.

Chan, M. (2022). *Digital Reality: The Body and Digital Technologies*. New York: Bloomsbury Academic.

Clark, P. A. (2021, November 15). The Metaverse Has Already Arrived. Here's What It Actually Means. *Time*, https://time.com/6116826/what-is-the-metaverse/.

Duffy, C. (2021, August 12). Why Silicon Valley Is Betting on Making this Dystopian Sci-fi Idea a Reality. *CNN*, https://edition.cnn.com/2021/08/08/tech/metaverse-explainer/index.html.

Faber, T. (2022, March 8). Why Gamers are Sceptical of Zuckerberg's Metaverse. *Financial Times*, https://www.ft.com/content/0c0e45dc-b0df-4a1a-8dd0-70668ce64a99.

Hackl, C. (2020, July 5). The Metaverse is Coming and It's a Very Big Deal. *Forbes*, https://www.forbes.com/sites/cathyhackl/2020/07/05/the-metaverse-is-coming--its-a-very-big-deal/?sh=4df2bc2b440f.

Hackl, C., Lueth, D. and Di Bartolo, T. (2022). *Navigating the Metaverse: A Guide to Limitless Possibilities in a Web 3.0 World*. Hoboken: Wiley.

Holmes, A. (2021, June 24). It's Time for Brands to Embrace the Metaverse. *Campaign Live*, https://www.campaignlive.co.uk/article/its-time-brands-embrace-metaverse/1720171.

Kelly, N. (2021, August 9). What is the Metaverse? A High-Tech Plan to Facebookify the World. *The Conversation*, https://theconversation.com/what-is-the-metaverse-a-high-tech-plan-to-facebookify-the-world-165326.

Koss, H. (2020, July 21). Are You Ready for the Metaverse? *Built In*, https://builtin.com/media-gaming/what-is-metaverse.

Mantegna, M. (2021, June 10). The Metaverse: A Brave, New (Virtual) World. *Medium*, https://medium.com/berkman-klein-center/the-metaverse-a-brave-new-virtual-world-2f040cbae7d4.

Morse, A. and Stein, S. (2022, January 21). The Metaverse is Just Getting Started: Here's What You Need to Know. *CNet*, https://www.cnet.com/tech/services-and-software/the-metaverse-is-everywhere-heres-what-you-need-to-know/.

Murphy, H. (2022, January 18). Facebook Patents Reveal How It Intends to Cash in on the Metaverse. *Financial Times*, https://www.ft.com/content/76d40aac-034e-4e0b-95eb-c5d34146f647.

Murray, J. H. (2020). Virtual/Reality: How to Tell the Difference. *Journal of Visual Culture*, 19(1), 11–27.

Oi, M. (2021, December 23). Is this the World's Largest Fashion Show? *BBC*, https://www.bbc.com/news/business-59558921.

Rooksby, M., McLeod, H. J. and Fururashi, T. (2020, October 29). Hikikomori: Understanding the People who Choose to Live in Extreme Isolation. *The Conversation*, https://theconversation.com/hikikomori-understanding-the-people-who-choose-to-live-in-extreme-isolation-148482.

Snider, M. (2021, April 21). From Minecraft to Zoom Calls, We've All Spent Much of the Pandemic on Our Screens. But Are We Ready for the Metaverse? *USA Today*, https://eu.usatoday.com/in-depth/tech/2021/04/21/minecraft-roblox-fortnite-nft-creating-metaverse/7000381002/.

Srnicek, N. (2017). *Platform Capitalism*. Cambridge: Polity Press.

Takahashi, D. (2021, June 30). The Metaverse ETF Will Let You Invest in Stocks that are the Internet's Future. *Venture Beat*, https://venturebeat.com/2021/06/30/the-metaverse-eft-will-let-you-invest-in-stocks-that-are-the-internets-future/.

The Economist. (2021, November 21). Don't Mock the Metaverse, https://www.economist.com/leaders/dont-mock-the-metaverse/21806354.

Threekit. (n.d.). Virtual Products and NFTs in the Metaverse. https://www.threekit.com/how-to-sell-virtual-products-in-the-metaverse.

Vaidhyanathan, S. (2018). *Anti-Social Media: How Facebook Disconnects Us and Undermines Democracy*. Oxford: Oxford University Press.

van Dijck, J., Poell, T. and de Waal, M. (2018). *The Platform Society: Public Values in a Connective World*. Oxford: Oxford University Press.

Virgilio, D. (2022, February 9). What Comparisons between *Second Life* and the Metaverse Miss. *Slate*, https://slate.com/technology/2022/02/second-life-metaverse-facebook-comparisons.html.

Volpicelli, G. (2021). The Shapeshifting Cam Girl Rewriting the Rules of Digital Porn. *Wired*, https://www.wired.com/story/cam-girl-face-morph-digital-porn/.

Wiederhold, B. K. (2022). Ready (or Not) Player One: Initial Musings on the Metaverse. *Cyberpsychology, Behavior, and Social Networking*, 25(1), 1–2.

Wiener, A. (2022, January 4). Money in the Metaverse. *The New Yorker*, https://www.newyorker.com/news/letter-from-silicon-valley/money-in-the-metaverse.

Winters, T. (2021). *The Metaverse: Prepare Now for the Next Big Thing!* Independently published.

Zhou, M., Leenders, M. A. A. M. and Cong, L. M. (2018). Ownership in the Virtual World and the Implications for Long-Term User Innovation Success. *Technovation*, 78, 56–65.

Zickgraf, R. (2021, September 25). Mark Zuckerberg's "Metaverse" Is a Dystopian Nightmare. *Jacobin*, https://www.jacobinmag.com/2021/09/facebook-zuckerberg-metaverse-stephenson-big-tech.

2 Why Now?

From Mediatisation to Virtualisation

The capacity to immerse is natural to humans and can be traced back at least to literature. Nevertheless, more recently, there has been a shift to turn online as much of daily life as possible, ultimately leading to the dominance of digital media logics across the whole society. A corollary is, then, the centrality of data collection and analytics in daily life, meaning that human presence is increasingly inseparable from algorithms and other digital artefacts. In this way, conditions are created for turning almost the entirety of human life into data. Such datafication, nevertheless, does not take place independently – instead, it primarily takes place through platforms as key units of social life and economic activity. And, while platformisation is already changing societies in a way that is comparable with the transformations brought about by industrialisation and electrification, its full potential to datafy and structure daily lives can only be realised through the metaverse. This is why the latter must be seen as the next stage of platformisation – an *evolution* of today's technologically mediated world and not a revolution.

2.1 Mediatisation and the Immersed Individual

Undergirding the metaverse is, of course, virtual reality, understood in a broader sense than a single experience but, instead, as a multiplicity of virtual worlds. As such, it must involve the fundamental attributes of being interactive, computer-generated, and immersive to the extent that '[i]nstead of showing you a two-dimensional screen, VR immerses you in a three-dimensional world you can see and hear as if you existed within it' (Chalmers 2022: xii). As such, virtual reality is sometimes credited with exceeding mere escapism and containing the potential of being 'a full-bloodied environment for living a genuine life' (Chalmers 2022: xvii). Of course, in order to *become* genuine life, the metaverse would need much more than simply immersive experiences: it would also need to have the *infrastructure* that

DOI: 10.4324/9781003355861-2

supports everyday life, including economic, cultural, educational, social, and other offerings. That would also necessitate an accumulation of a critical mass of service and opportunity providers, as well as ordinary users, that would be within easy reach without hopping from one platform to another, leading to market concentration in a handful of all-encompassing platforms.

It must be kept in mind that immersion in imaginary worlds is a long-standing human faculty, clearly illustrated, for example, by the practice of reading books, whereby readers co-create the story-worlds by visualising the unfolding plot (Stiegler 2021: 111). In film, we still participate by way of imagining what is beyond the screen and emotionally investing in the story, but the freedom of co-creation is already limited owing to the visual nature of the medium. In a way, development of virtual experiences is about corporate actors making use of the natural human capacity to dream and imagine – by conditioning, framing, and packaging it into discrete consumable and datafiable bits (Stiegler 2021: 14). The metaverse would still be co-created and co-imagined, particularly in terms of socially interactive experiences, but simultaneously more and less constrained, from an imagination point of view, than film: on the one hand, the metaverse would be less open to imagination because the entirety of the user's environment would be manufactured, thus leaving little room for involvement, but, on the other hand, while in a book or in a film the story is scripted, in the metaverse, the users would be within the events as they unfold. That freedom would still not be absolute, though, as it would be contingent upon the devices, user agreements and community policies, and the AI tools generating and moderating the virtual environments (not to mention that at least some of the avatars with whom one interacts would likely be synthetic AI-powered agents). Ultimately, then, the scope left to the natural human capacity to imagine would end up dependent on corporate business models, aesthetic choices, licensing agreements, etc.

Yet another variable helping normalise a potential shift towards a digital-first life is the already manifest acute pressure to digitise and otherwise translate into online-first as many services and experiences as possible – not just in the private sector but in the public sector as well, to the extent that citizenship today is becoming increasingly digital by default (Syvertsen 2020: 7). Ultimately, the increasing penetration of and reliance on digital media and other technologies involve a deepening of connectedness and interdependence among not only individuals but also multiple entities involved in the process (Hepp 2020: 85). In fact, today's world is already permeated by media of various descriptions. As Couldry and Hepp (2017: 15) observe, the social world is '*changed* in its dynamics and structure by the role that media continuously (indeed recursively) play in its construction'. It is increasingly evident that societies are becoming mediatised, i.e.

submitted to, or dependent on, media logic (Hjarvard 2008: 113; see also Hepp, Hjarvard and Lundby 2015: 321).

The process of mediatisation is best understood in terms of direct translation from transformations *within* the media domain to transformations of culture and society as a whole (Hepp 2020: 3–4). The ever-deepening condition of mediatisation is thus one 'in which all elements of our social world are intricately related to digital media and their underlying infrastructures' (Hepp 2020: 5). Moreover, this process is increasingly automated and subjected to constant data collection, processing, and utilisation (Andrejevic 2020: 41). Hence, it comes as no surprise that, as Gekker and Hind (2020: 1415–1416) stress, the backbone of day-to-day existence is increasingly formed of 'a growing number of "smart-" and data-driven technologies in which user surveillance is stated as necessary precondition for its operation'. In this way, the capacity to collect, integrate, and use data to surreptitiously build and shape daily experiences and conditions for action becomes the new domain of power brokerage (Ytre-Arne and Das 2021: 780).

There is also potentially a change in user outlook – if not consciously, then at least as a matter of broader culture: as Debrabander (2020: 11) notes, '[a] striking feature of the digital age is that we [...] hand over personal information to those who watch us', leading to the emergence of 'a confessional culture'. Of course, the extent to which this is a properly informed and freely chosen handing over of data or simply a matter of there being no meaningful alternative to (implicitly or explicitly) agreeing with data collection and processing owing to the digital integration of today's world is another matter. Nevertheless, the more deeply this confessionalism (understood broadly – not merely as intentional disclosure but also as simply remaining *passively* aware of collection and processing taking place) becomes engrained in everyday practices and routines and the more used people become to trading data for the conveniences of tailored products and experiences, the more difficult it would become to enact any change (Debrabander 2020: 158). The preceding is, however, certainly not an independently occurring phenomenon: as Couldry and Mejias (2019: 7) stress, there is a fair amount of intentionality and vested interest in such digital transformations since 'human life, and particularly human social life, is increasingly being constructed *so that* it generates data from which profit can be extracted'. The goal is to eliminate the opacity of human behaviour through the use of algorithms and data, exerting power on human experience accordingly (Aho and Duffield 2020: 190; see also Zuboff 2019; Fisher 2022). Again, this would be particularly manifest in the metaverse as a more controllable and malleable environment than the current blend of digital and physical life.

Once the data collection and analytics infrastructure is set in place, curation takes shape not just in relatively crude ways, such as structuration of experience though direct content governance. A more subtle way of achieving the same inheres in various recommender systems that increasingly undergird choices made in today's world, ostensibly to allow users to transcend the limitations of their human nature in identifying, evaluating, and ranking preferences (see e.g. Domingos 2017: 45). In this way, the networked digital environments in which individuals frequently find themselves are best seen as located at the intersection between data and algorithms, thereby fundamentally altering our understanding of human subjectivity from autonomous to a distributed one (see e.g. Dogruel, Facciorusso and Stark 2020: 1; Fisher 2022). Under such circumstances, human interrelatedness with the economic-technological systems of the day becomes the norm. And, as such systems only grow in their scope and engulfing of individuals within mediatised environments and activities, the metaverse is simply the next natural step within the process.

Even in crudely practical terms, with ever-increasing surveillance for the purpose of data collection and progressive reliance on automated decision-making based on that data, human actions and choices can no longer be fully attributed to the independent agency of an autonomous self, thereby 'removing the boundaries that previously existed between internal life and external forces' (Couldry and Mejias 2019: 7; see also Fisher 2022). Similarly, for Nowotny (2022: 20), '[w]e become part of a fine-tuned and interconnected predictive system that is dynamically closed upon itself'. Under such circumstances, agency is evidently shared, whereby interactions with the world and others become interactions among data-based systems, regardless of whether we are aware of it or not, with such systems managing content, contacts, and dealings of various sorts (Domingos 2017: 269; see also Dogruel, Facciorusso and Stark 2020: 3). Indeed, then, data and the tools used to make sense of it and to (inter)act accordingly become the ultimate moderators of contemporary existence (Herian 2021: 2), making the manufactured and permanently rendered world of the metaverse less exceptional than might otherwise seem.

The above changes also have a clear effect on the human self. Perhaps the most visible manifestation has been the opening up of the human self and reduction of the private sphere, with a growing expectation that one is 'available for interaction on digital media platforms and even [...] a certain pressure to represent itself on these platforms' (Couldry and Hepp 2017: 145) – a trend clearly related to the emergence of the 'confessional culture' mentioned above. This also holds a clue to further transformations: the presentative, or performative, nature of this publicised self. As Oliver stresses (2020: 91), '[o]ur human identity does not end at the boundary of our bodies and our minds are deeply connected to one another', with new technologies having enabled the expansion of such networks so that 'our power and reach to influence others has dramatically increased'. That relationality, nevertheless, does not need to be face-to-face – it can be, and nowadays typically is, mediated – even virtually so.

In fact, the self as such is rendered dependent on – indeed, inseparable from – both the platforms on which it is performed, and the attention and recognition received from others – users are thus tied within such digital-first ecosystems through 'affective feedback loops' (Boler and Davis 2018: 83–84). Here one can easily observe 'the blurring of the distinction between reality and virtuality' as well as 'the blurring of the distinction between human, machine and nature', collectively associated with 'the shift from the primacy of entities to the primacy of interactions' (The Onlife Initiative 2015: 7). In that sense, one should agree with Pedersen and Iliadis (2020: xxiii) who stress that humans today exist as 'data-blended bodies', i.e. bodies that are permanently enmeshed with the data generated *by* them and deemed to be relevant *to* them.

As the above infrastructure for enmeshment is always-on, so are the unfolding and evolution of the body–data relation (Lupton 2020a: 54). Similarly, Lury and Wakeford (2012: 2) proceed to describe the social world as one that is constantly happening, only manifesting itself in terms of 'ongoingness, relationality, contingency, and sensuousness'. To this effect, a core characteristic of today's world is it being an 'intricate mix between offline and online universes' (Dewandre 2020: 3). In this sense, one must also agree with Tucker (2018: 39–40) that '[w]e are not made to feel *by* digital technologies, we feel *with* them', ultimately forming 'meshworks of entangled lines of body, data and technology' (for a similar argument, see also Bender and Broderick 2021). The shared temporality that thereby emerges has 'the now' as its central point of concern, creating an experience that is 'stretched and condensed in various ways' (Coleman 2018: 68). Such uneven renderings of experience are best understood in terms of patterns and actuations of data that ultimately are translated into meaningful structurations of the world, such as instances of content moderation. In a similar fashion, following Deuze (2012), everything – from beliefs to emotions, relationships to memories, and even distinctions between right and wrong – can only be imagined as deeply intertwined with media, indeed, inseparable from them. More generally speaking, the various distinctions and antinomies that have been easy categories for orientation, such as real and artificial, physical and digital, the self and the other, are losing the explanatory value they once – if ever – had.

Notably, in today's digital-first world, one could confidently say that 'the idea of the self is defined by its actions within mediated experiences'

(Stiegler 2021: 88). Simultaneously, though, the same also holds the other way round: the way users construct their virtual selves has an impact on both professional and personal relationships and the social roles to be played (Stiegler 2021: 168). Hence, the relationship between the offline and the mediated self is an interactive one. However, the representational aspect of avatars cannot go unquestioned – after all, these are 'idolized versions of ourselves' that we immerse ourselves in, ultimately transcending 'the limits of physical reality' (Stiegler 2021: 172). In this way, the authenticity of avatar-to-avatar interactions within virtual environments is likely to become a major point of debate, with the potential for both toxicity and disinformation featuring heavily.

Typically, both casual and intimate relations have depended on another person, on there being 'someone to amplify and reflect your experience, to reciprocate and compound it'; through the mediation of digital technologies, meanwhile, it is becoming possible for this other party to be an avatar, with or without an actual human person behind it – particularly when one pairs the growing capacities of AI with the feeling of presence induced by virtual experiences (Rubin 2020: 8). In other words, having meaningful interactions with an automated (AI-based) virtual agent that presents itself through an avatar is by no means inconceivable. Moreover, such interactions could potentially have similar, or even identical, effects to interacting with an avatar that stands in for a human person. What matters, then, is affective interplay rather than fixed attributes.

The seamless translation from users to data and from data back to the users (affecting user world-perception and behaviour in the meantime) leads to the rise of an 'attention economy', manifested by a 'have it now' culture of 'real-time instant gratification' (Evans 2016: 577). For Dahlgren (2018: 26), meanwhile, the current changes regarding knowledge and attention are 'historical', with daily practices being 'characterised by high velocity and dizzying excess', particularly within the digital domain. Similarly, as Syvertsen (2020: 6) stresses, '[t]he scarcest commodity is people's attention', with the latter implying a clear need for new technologies that can be used 'to capture it, holding on to it and earning money from it'. Crucially, attention allocation has also become intertwined with the inner workings of digital platforms: on the one hand, there is a clear scarcity of attention as an ever-growing onslaught of content, experiences, and other triggers are constantly vying for it while, on the other hand, there is an ever more elaborate push for attaining any use value possible out of the attention that *is* captured (Doyle and Roda 2019: 1–2). Constant innovation is thereby a natural and unavoidable corollary to the fragmented and oversaturated media environment (Syvertsen 2020: 26). As will be shown later, the metaverse constitutes a significant improvement in terms of attention and data capture, with the virtual self becoming an agent of datafication of both themselves and of others.

The keyword, nevertheless, ought to be seamlessness – not just in terms of the avatar and its behaviour or interactions with other avatars (representing both humans and artificial personalities) but also with regard to the broader interactions with the digital environment: just like users are already used to AI-driven recommendations and content moderation based on their own and others' data (Hamilton et al. 2021: 1508), in the metaverse this would amount to constant adaptation of the totality of one's environment – most likely, with commercial interests, such as product placement, featuring heavily. Both reality and, largely, user expectation now tend to be premised upon the adaptation and customisation of anything the user encounters. Such customisation is completely different from the user themselves tinkering with different options – instead, that tinkering is performed automatically because of surveillance and forecasting (Dogruel, Facciorusso and Stark 2020: 2–3). Seamlessness is, therefore, crucial for the retention of attention as, otherwise, users would turn (and give away their data) elsewhere.

The metaverse also tends to break traditional conventions associated with media content consumption: while conventional wisdom has involved a separation of the content and the viewer in the form of a screen (Dooley 2021: 26–27), virtual experiences are about presence *within*. In fact, user experience of content dwarfs in importance the content itself (Bender and Broderick 2021). Simultaneously, a crucial feature that inheres in virtual experiences is that of perceived proximity to a place in which one is immersed, regardless of the geographical distance or the place itself having been completely manufactured, leading to the development of a strong emotional connection to what is being experienced and the narrative that is unfolding, be it structured (as in, for example, VR journalism), semi-structured (e.g. games), or completely free-flowing as it tends to be in unstructured social spaces – and the more responsive the environment is, the stronger the sense of being there becomes (Kukkakorpi and Pantti 2021: 786–787). The resulting immersion prevents the user from moving elsewhere and locks them in instead, meaning that the battle for dominance in the metaverse will be a battle for the most total immersion.

Ideally (from the standpoint of the creators of virtual worlds), one should forget the very fact of the medium being in place, perceiving the content in front of one's eyes as if it was immediately present, so that the user is cognitively and mentally transported to that place (Bolter, Engberg and MacIntyre 2021: 75). As users feel present in the virtual world, virtual reality itself is turned into a 'visceral medium' which could be the source of empathy but could also trigger psychological harm in the case of encountering intense negative experiences; likewise, such depth of user involvement also creates the conditions for manipulation of choices and behaviours (Mabrook 2021: 210). To this effect, it might not be overly far-fetched to assert that, from the standpoint of the experiencing subject at least, 'virtual reality is genuine reality' that should not be dismissed as mere simulation or an experience second to the 'real' world – instead, proponents allege, virtual realities 'can be first-class realities' (Chalmers 2022: xvii). Consequently, such environments would be on par with conventional reality if not better – in fact, even a potential emigration destination from a degraded world (Chalmers 2022: xiv). Oddly, though, consideration of the ethics of such escape, either as a mass strategy or as fantasies of some technology CEOs, is hard to come by.

Still, while discussions of feasibility and immersiveness typically focus on user-facing technologies, such as headsets or haptics, an oft-forgotten question is that of infrastructure: for a fully immersive metaverse, connection speeds would have to be improved, likely going beyond the capacity of existing network infrastructure and connection standards, while a vast array of new devices would have to be manufactured as well in order to support the computing power needs of real-time rendering and the storage needs of virtual world data (Arcidiacono 2022; Ball 2022). All this would come at a great cost not only financially but also environmentally, in terms of pollution, energy consumption, and resource extraction. For this reason, an escape from the messed-up physical world into a virtual one would result in the latter being even more messed up.

2.2 Platformisation, Datafication, and the Technology–Experience Nexus

Interactions among users already are, and increasingly will be even more, dependent on devices, networks, and platforms operated by large technology companies and subjected to their terms and conditions, thereby significantly reducing the autonomy of human relationships (Lemley and Volokh 2018: 1056). In that sense, interactions lose their independent importance and are better conceived as a joint partaking in a 'social factory' the purpose of which is value creation in the form of data (Kaplan 2019: 1950). Indeed, one could claim that it is no longer possible to 'think of humanity as distinct from technology anymore' (Stiegler 2021: 203). Crucial to the functioning of today's economy is the intertwining of people, contexts, and the capacity to datafy and analyse them as the locus of value, cutting across almost any conceivable sector of activity, from private to political to economic and beyond (Andrejevic 2020: 97; Brevini 2020: 1). The expectation, therefore, is that of a society in which interpretation is no longer necessary owing to the (supposed or actual) accuracy of live data collection and analysis (Krasmann 2020: 2099). The technology companies, therefore, are extremely reluctant to leave anything to chance.

The societal condition described above is perhaps best captured through the concept of platformisation. According to van Dijck, Poell and de Waal (2018: 19), this concept 'refers to the way in which entire societal actors are transforming as a result of the mutual shaping of online connectors and complementors'. Platforms also act as gatekeepers, enabling some content, connections, behaviours, creative practices, etc. but not others (Poell, Nieborg and Duffy 2022: 7–8). In a similar manner, Couldry and Mejias (2019: 25) describe platforms in general as 'structured online spaces, made possible through elaborate software, that offer services of various sorts: a space to sell things, meet people, share information, find specialist resources, and so on' but in a manner that is wholly contingent upon the deeper underlying goal – extraction of data. As a result, then, it is part and parcel of the typical platform business model that they 'operate as multiway data auctions, linking users, data buyers and users, and of course the platform itself' (Couldry and Mejias 2019: 25). This, however, does not happen in a neutral fashion. Following Srnicek (2017: 42–43), while platforms may have first appeared as purely technical solutions to the problems and obstacles inherent in handling data, ultimately, they 'became an efficient way to monopolise, extract, analyse, and use' the ever-growing troves of data, generated not just on a daily or hourly basis but every fraction of a second. As platform companies are constantly in the business of looking for ever new linkages (and, therefore, data streams) to be added into the mix and for new – more efficient – ways to extract data from the existing ones, their attention to the metaverse seems perfectly understandable.

In fact, platformisation is to be seen as a large-scale, all-encompassing process – one comparable with industrialisation or electrification, that is, not merely a standalone matter but a transformative force that reconstitutes entire societies; what needs to be kept in mind, though, is that this process is taking place under the tight grip of a limited number of technology companies that now 'increasingly control the gateways to all Internet traffic, data circulation, and content distribution', thereby 'making entire societies dependent on their systems' (van Dijck 2021: 2802; see also Srnicek 2017: 45). This platform power emerges not only as a matter of data and user aggregation but also with regard to various content development toolkits that enable add-ons and extensions to existing platforms while simultaneously setting the conditions for participation in and experience of the digital sections of daily lives and locking both users and developers therein (Blanke and Pybus 2020: 11; see also Poell, Nieborg and Duffy 2022). The latter is particularly visible in some of the already existing proto-metaverses, such as *Roblox*.

The grip and power exerted by platform companies as well as their capacity to accumulate and analyse user data to provide ever more tailored experiences and content lead to increasing market concentration and, likewise, severe limitations to any competitors entering the market (Poell, Nieborg and Duffy 2022: 42–43). Crucially, platforms rely on what is known as 'network effects', whereby 'the more numerous the users who use the platform, the more valuable that platform becomes for everyone else' and the higher the cost of opting out (Srnicek 2017: 45). But, once in, content creators (and other users of platforms) need to constantly remain aware of any changes in the business models and operating practices of the platform(s) on which they are dependent so as not to lose their audiences overnight (Poell, Nieborg and Duffy 2022: 180). This is an increasingly precarious position to be in, forcing users to constantly be on high alert to stay on top of their game.

Given platform evolution, development, and expansion, virtualisation must be seen as the logical next step. This would imply a shift of focus from relatively plain societal interactions to a significantly more all-encompassing ambition to surround the user with and immerse them in platform-based content and experiences within which interactions would be datafied by default. Most importantly, though, such virtual worlds would be 'owned and controlled by the companies that create them' (Gault 2021). Hence, as platformisation already denotes a shift in power towards technology companies, the metaverse is going to extend it further and make it more all-encompassing. Such virtual worlds would not be separate from the offline dimension: as Stiegler (2021: 53) notes, immersion has the tendency to remain powerful and retain tangible effects on the self even after the experience in question has ended, being 'highly influential as physical and psychological sensations that make it difficult to distinguish between the physical and the mediated'. In a way, then, the two realities become bridged – or even entangled – within one's mind. After all, immersion is not merely passive consumption of media content but, instead, an active process (Stiegler 2021: 79). In other words, with regard to immersion, there is co-constitution between virtual platform content and user perception. This is, at least in part, also the reason why, even when the virtual environment is far from photorealistic, the level of immersion is still high (Stiegler 2021: 92). Such an active participatory role that users take upon them also is key to the success of platforms as users self-enclose within digital spaces through continuous engagement (Stiegler 2021: 101). In this way, humans, devices, and platform businesses become part of one datafication engine.

Notably, virtual experiences are more immersive and all-encompassing than earlier platform environments (such as social media), primarily owing to the feeling of presence. Following Rubin (2020: 124) definition, '[p]resence is what happens when your brain is so fooled by a virtual experience that it triggers your body to respond as though the experience were real' (Rubin 2020: 124). Even memories arising from virtual experiences have a tendency to feel embodied, even though they have nothing to do with the physical world (Rubin 2020: 138). Hence, the feeling of presence increases the effects of any virtual experiences. Crucially, presence is all about the here and now, occurring 'during an encounter with technology' (Stiegler 2021: 49). This increases the stakes for content creators aiming to immerse and retain users as less-than-gratifying experiences would simply lead to users drifting somewhere else – there is only a here-and-now chance of capturing and holding on to the user. The key challenge would thus be to create an environment that is constantly adaptive and gratifying. This is being done not only by human content creators but also through the use of AI to, first, aid in content curation and, subsequently, partake in the creative process itself to the point where AI will 'merge with immersive technologies to create *all-surrounding media experiences governed with the help of machine learning*' (Stiegler 2021: 217). Hence, the digital world should be particularly effective in constantly making itself liked.

Of course, the capacity to surround and immerse users does not arise from nothing. It comes from one of the hallmarks of platformisation – datafication, whereby data collection becomes 'an economic and design imperative' (Tulloch and Johnson 2022: 933). Datafication also pertains to one of the idols of today: transparency. In effect, while transparency (of governments, of algorithms, etc.) is typically seen as a tool for greater autonomy and safety, in this case, it involves rendering users completely transparent to online platforms (Adams 2021). While such transparency is sometimes given a positive spin as a way to obtain 'actionable insights' to better serve users (see e.g. Hackl, 2020, Lueth and Di Bartolo 2022: 81), the privacy risks here are more than clear. Just like one of the key elements of platforms' power is their ability to collect vast amounts of user data and turn it to tailored content (in fact, the effectiveness of data collection and use is at the heart of platform competition), the metaverse is a data-intensive undertaking. In fact, it is even more data-intensive than, for example, social media, necessitating extensive user tracking, including, in addition to usage data, biometric data for the purpose of both responding to user actions and movements and representing them as an avatar; while, on the surface, such data collection is purely functional, the richness of the information collected 'allows companies to gain a deeper understanding of users' behaviour, which in turn can be used to tailor advertising campaigns in an exceptionally targeted way' (Ahmad and Corovic 2022; see also Bolter, Engberg and MacIntyre 2021). In fact, one could say that the metaverse enables a totalisation of surveillance, whereby literally everything one does and every reaction one has are being tracked and analysed (Bolter, Engberg and MacIntyre 2021).

Surveillance is both necessary (for surreptitious adaptation of the virtual environment so that everything is intuitive and immersive) and extremely lucrative as both the knowledge of users and the capacity to dynamically and constantly shape the virtual world that they encounter are easily commercialised. Of course, for any platform, knowing users well in order to supply content that they are bound to like is not an end but a means: it helps attract more users and retain existing ones, increase time spent on the platform (or using services provided through the platform), and thus collect more data; the ultimate aim, nevertheless, is to sell either the knowledge thus generated or the user attention that has thereby been attracted – of the right audiences to the right customers (van Dijck, Poell and de Waal 2018: 35). Ultimately, the activities of platform companies should be interpreted in light of their aim to 'expand their collecting and processing of data to track and predict an ever wider variety of users' performances, sentiments, transactions, informal exchanges, and activities' so that any latent monetary value could be squeezed out (van Dijck, Poell and de Waal 2018: 36; see also Lupton 2020b: 8).

Platform companies represent a powerful combination of digital technologies and the profit motive, whereby the transformation of behaviour into data and then the packaging of the latter into prediction products can, as if magically, predict or, rather, shape future trends and behaviours (Seubert and Becker 2019: 933). Indeed, there is a fine line between prediction and shaping – as Nowotny (2022: 19) stresses, algorithms are less predictive than they are performative, i.e. they are capable of making happen what they predict – a kind of self-fulfilling prophecy (see also Fisher 2022: 19, 32). This power to make things happen as opposed to merely foreseeing them also has a clear dimension of power and control. In fact, making things happen can also be a very explicit role, particularly in the more ostensibly benevolent applications (that typically manifest themselves as some form of algorithmic decision-making for the proclaimed social or personal good). From this point of view, the more power and function are delegated to algorithmic systems of governance, the more value is created for all – even (or particularly) if it comes at the expense of human agency (see e.g. Mayer-Schönberger and Ramge 2019; Sundar 2020: 77; for criticism, see e.g. Lupton 2020b).

Simultaneously, platforms signify an important step towards automatisation of setting norms, standards, and frameworks for encountering the world around us: if, previously, the media providing such experiences were, first and foremost, human-created, produced, and targeted to a specific market (from oral storytelling to writing and painting to digital media), now they are increasingly algorithm-curated (see e.g. van Dijck, Poell and de Waal 2018: 40; Fisher 2022). It must be kept in mind that platformisation largely takes place and develops within the intersection of the human and the non-human (van Dijck 2021: 4). This leads to an important transformation of world-experience: the latter becomes morphing and adaptive but also individualised to the maximum feasible extent. While this does not have to be explicitly manipulative or otherwise harmful, it nevertheless further extends some of the conundrums inherent in social media, particularly with regard to content moderation – by adding the issue of content *generation* on top of the matter. Here, again, matters of the interests and criteria under which such governance processes take place remain just as, if not more, contested than with regard to conventional social media.

Nevertheless, the datafication of digital media use – which, given the ever-expanding spectrum of various digital 'smart' technologies and the advent of the metaverse, increasingly means the datafication of the entirety of daily life – has a further, much broader, set of concerns, pertaining to the societal position of technology companies and their historical role. Crucially, extraction – primarily of natural resources – has been a key feature of modernity; correspondingly, the current period can be seen as one marked by a specific kind of extraction – that of data. Some of the more lenient authors tend to portray ever more pervasive datafication as some form of exchange in which 'customers pay not just with their wallets but also with their data' (Siggelkow and Terwiesch 2019: 103), thereby trying to reframe the matter as a question of value for money (and data). However, the often covert, pervasive, and non-exclusionary way in which much, if not most, of the collection takes place insinuates a more one-sided way in which audiences are *acted on*. Indeed, as Velkova and Kaun (2019: 6) observe, what we are witnessing today is 'algorithmic conversion of audiences into objects to mine'. This one-way objectification of populations definitely has a disempowering effect, turning individuals from social actors to entities being *acted on*.

For mining and extraction (including of data) to confer a competitive advantage, they must be done to the exclusion of others. The idea of exclusion is also deeply rooted in modern thought and practice. State sovereignty, for example, has been understood as the exercise of political control at the expense of other similar entities. Platforms, likewise, practise exclusion within *their own specific domain* – control of digital personal and economic behaviour and the data thus generated. For this reason, then, it comes as no surprise that platformisation 'has upended the once popular ideal of a universal and neutral Internet that connects the world' (van Dijck 2021: 2). Simultaneously, platforms are also constantly expanding their home turf by spreading across sectors (a single company having either native presence or acquisitions across e.g. social media, search, autonomous vehicles, Internet of Things, etc.); in this way, the scope and profitability of extraction can be increased significantly by integrating and applying multiple data streams (van Dijck 2021: 9–10). There is little reason to believe that the dynamics would change with the arrival of the metaverse.

Hence, what the metaverse signifies is both a continuation and an intensification of the present trends. Here one must agree, in principle at least, with Lupton's (2020c) assertion that every new extension of technology into everyday life has one main goal – extended datafication. Just as Mosco (2017: 41) criticises the term 'Internet of Things' as an obfuscation – for putting emphasis on things while ultimately it is still about people (users) and their data – the experiential aspect of the metaverse could be seen as simply an excuse and a cover for ever more pervasive data extraction. Indeed, the various keywords around smartness, adaptation, sensing capacities, etc. function not only as legitimation strategies but also as clear indicators of the pervasive scope of surveillance: gathering data from the entire environment and making surreptitious decisions in the background that – because of their 'smartness' – often acquire significant autonomy from the human owner but, arguably, not from the businesses that have created the products in question; in fact, in more than one way, the humans here are simultaneously the owners and the owned (see, generally, Zuboff 2019: 239; Andrejevic 2020: 116). And while, in the physical space, such conditioning is generally limited by environmental factors and unpredictabilities that can distract users or make them more difficult to reach, the metaverse opens a completely malleable and controllable domain with much greater predictability than could be possible, even with the most accurate of data, in the physical world. Similar tendencies are already visible in a domain that has traditionally been known for its autonomy and irreverence – play; after all, the contemporary gaming industry is fundamentally based around the extraction of as much data as possible not only for the personalisation and optimisation of gameplay but also for further commercial use (Tulloch and Johnson 2022). This can certainly be seen as a blueprint for future (no doubt even more extensive) datafication in the metaverse.

An even more pervasive example of the same is the spread and normalisation of wearable devices of various kinds that contribute to 'the production of legible, quantifiable and consumable bodies' (Sandvik 2020: 2017). On the one hand, body tracking and promotion of the quantified self are an extension of datafication tendencies: as Pedersen and Iliadis (2020: xxiii) observe, '[t]he telos or end goal of smart technologies is to have every object connected to the internet' – and that includes every human body – leading to the creation of not merely the Internet of Things but, instead, 'the Internet of People'. Hence, it comes as no surprise that, for Lupton (2020a:

52) among others, the effective mode of existence today is as 'assemblages of flesh–device–data generated by wearable technologies'. Simultaneously, though, individuals cannot avoid this pervasive (and invasive) computing even if they decide to refuse wearables as they are always sharing space with sensing technologies of various kinds; in the end, opting out is, literally, not an option (Lupton 2020a: 52). On the other hand, though, it must be reiterated that the metaverse goes beyond the simple increase in effectiveness of collecting data that is already there – it is about both datafication by default (as the necessary precondition for using the associated hardware) and the creation of conditions for collection of data that would not normally exist (such as purposive creation of virtual experiences to generate and collect specific kinds of data).

What the above demonstrates is the need to manufacture data: although the talk is often of data as a 'resource', unlike natural resources, such as oil, data does not simply occur; rather, it is 'a by-product of *social interactions* that are mediated by digital technologies' at the design and for the benefit of a third party (Couldry and Mejias 2019: 89). In this sense, two summands are necessary: some happening and an external mediation with a recording capacity. If there is just a happening, such as a face-to-face conversation, then, even though data is produced, it remains enclosed within the happening, being perceived solely through the senses of the participants. Likewise, even if external mediation exists, but without the capacity to capture and store data by and for third parties (for example, one person using binoculars to observe another person giving a signal), the threshold is not yet crossed either. Crucially, the happening in question is to be understood in the broadest sense possible and not just as interaction among humans; anything can be the source of data if there is someone or something to capture and record that data, and particularly if that capture is intentional, i.e. for their or somebody else's benefit.

The presence of an external self-interested party also signifies that, even though platforms may generate benefits to their users, such benefits are simply by-products of the broader practices of inter-platform competition; in order to retain or acquire a competitive edge, '[platforms] must intensify their extraction, analysis, and control of data' (Srnicek 2017: 97). This ultimately leads to what Andrejevic (2017: 893) calls '[t]he postpanoptic model of "total" – or environmental – surveillance': while the idea of the Panopticon had been premised on the *potential* of being observed *from a single centre* rather than the unavoidability thereof, current digital infrastructures enable both real-time (or very nearly so) data collection and analysis and, largely, the *certainty* of being observed *from multiple points (sensors) simultaneously*. Both the scale of the task and the speed necessary have a further implication: that of automation becoming a necessity

(Andrejevic 2017: 893). In this way, human subjection to the machines is not some kind of futuristic dystopian scenario so widespread in popular culture depicting robot revolts or artificial intelligence going awry but a much more banal and mundane daily presence.

Ultimately, a clear element of extraction *as* domination must be underscored. As Birhane (2020: 391) pinpoints, whereas, back in colonial times, power was primarily exerted as unilateral domination through reinventing the entire political, social, and economic order in a self-serving way, in the era of platforms and their algorithms, 'this control and domination occurs not through brute physical force but rather through invisible and nuanced mechanisms such as control of digital ecosystems and infrastructure'. That control can be nuanced and tailored owing to one of the main promises of algorithms – that they can offer 'a truer, richer, more precise knowledge about the world and about our self' (Fisher 2022: 10–11). Arguably, owing to the immense data requirements (extraction) and the complete malleability of the manufactured virtual environment (control), the metaverse is not only a manifestation but a concentration of power. Indeed, there is a growing emphasis in discussions on the socio-political effects of digital technologies on parallels between what could be called historical and digital colonialism (Hao and Swart 2022). Perhaps more emphatically than other recent scholarly contribution to this end, Couldry and Mejias (2019: x) assert that the entire digital-technological environment should be interpreted as 'the systematic attempt to turn all human lives and relations into inputs for the generation of profit' to the extent that '[h]uman experience, potentially every layer and aspect of it, is becoming the target of profitable extraction', thereby leading to '*colonization by data*'. In effect, then, what such algorithmic and data colonialism has in common with its historical form 'is the desire to dominate, monitor, and influence social, political, and cultural discourse through the control of core communication and infrastructure mediums' (Birhane 2020: 391). Therefore, user agency (and even the structural possibility thereof) is put into question as the essence of data-based algorithmic curation is all about the triggering of specific pre-planned user behaviours based on content that is strategically put forth to them by the online platforms through their own specifically coded architectures and infrastructures (van Dijck, Poell and de Waal 2018: 40–41).

Overall, then, the premises of the metaverse seem to be more evolutionary than revolutionary. As shown in the subsequent chapters, this does not preclude the metaverse from recreating or reinventing numerous aspects of everyday life. While it is important not to fall into the trap of various (economic, technological, etc.) determinisms, it would also be unwise to ignore the trends and tendencies in the introduction and development of the metaverse.

Bibliography

Adams, R. (2021). *Transparency: New Trajectories in Law*. London: Routledge.

Ahmad, I. and Corovic, T. (2022, January 25). Privacy in a Parallel Universe: The Metaverse. *Norton Rose Fulbright*, https://www.dataprotectionreport.com/2022/01/privacy-in-a-parallel-digital-universe-the-metaverse/.

Aho, B. and Duffield, R. (2020). Beyond Surveillance Capitalism: Privacy, Regulation and Big Data in Europe and China. *Economy and Society*, 49(2), 187–212.

Andrejevic, M. (2017). To Preempt a Thief. *International Journal of Communication*, 11, 879–896.

Andrejevic, M. (2020). *Automated Media*. London: Routledge.

Arcidiacono, A. (2022). Whatever the Metaverse *May* Be, It *Must* Be Sustainable. *Tech-i*, 51, 3.

Ball, M. (2022). *The Metaverse and How It will Revolutionize Everything*. New York: Liveright Publishing Corporation.

Bender, S. M. and Broderick, M. (2021). *Virtual Realities: Case Studies in Immersion and Phenomenology*. London: Palgrave Macmillan.

Birhane, A. (2020). Algorithmic Colonization of Africa. *Scripted*, 17(2), 389–409.

Blanke, T. and Pybus, J. (2020). The Material Conditions of Platforms: Monopolization Through Decentralization. *Social Media + Society*, doi: 10.1177/2056305120971632.

Boler, M. and Davis, E. (2018). The Affective Politics of the 'Post-Truth' Era: Feeling Rules and Networked Subjectivity. *Emotion, Space & Society*, 27, 75–85.

Bolter, J. D., Engberg, M. and MacIntyre, B. (2021). *Reality Media: Augmented and Virtual Reality*. Cambridge: The MIT Press.

Brevini, B. (2020). Black Boxes, not Green: Mythologizing Artificial Intelligence and Omitting the Environment. *Big Data & Society*, doi: 10.1177/2053951720935141.

Chalmers, D. J. (2022). *Reality +: Virtual Worlds and the Problems of Philosophy*. New York: W. W. Norton & Company.

Coleman, R. (2018). Social Media and the Materialisation of the Affective Present. In T. D. Sampson, S. Maddison and D. Ellis (eds.) *Affect and Social Media: Emotion, Mediation, Anxiety and Contagion* (pp. 67–75). London: Rowman & Littlefield.

Couldry, N. and Hepp, A. (2017). *The Mediated Construction of Reality*. Cambridge: Polity.

Couldry, N. and Mejias, U. A. (2019). *The Costs of Connection: How Data Is Colonizing Human Life and Appropriating It for Capitalism*. Stanford: Stanford University Press.

Dahlgren, P. (2018). Media, Knowledge and Trust: The Deepening Epistemic Crisis of Democracy. *Javnost – The Public*, 25(1), 20–27.

Debrabander, F. (2020). *Life After Privacy: Reclaiming Democracy in a Surveillance Society*. Cambridge: Cambridge University Press.

Deuze, M. (2012). *Media Life*. Malden: Polity.

Dewandre, N. (2020). Big Data: From Modern Fears to Enlightened and Vigilant Embrace of New Beginnings. *Big Data & Society*, doi: 10.1177/2053951720936708.

Dogruel, L., Facciorusso, D. and Stark, B. (2020). 'I'm Still the Master of the Machine'. Internet Users' Awareness of Algorithmic Decision-Making and their Perception of Its Effect in their Autonomy. *Information, Communication & Society*, doi: 10.1080/1369118X.2020.1863999.

Domingos, P. (2017). *The Master Algorithm: How the Quest for the Ultimate Learning Machine Will Remake Our World*. London: Penguin Books.

Dooley, K. (2021). *Cinematic Virtual Reality: A Critical Study of 21st Century Approaches and Practices*. London: Palgrave Macmillan.

Doyle, W. and Roda, C. (2019). Introduction. In W. Doyle and C. Roda (eds.) *Communication in the Era of Attention Scarcity* (pp. 1–6). London: Palgrave Macmillan.

Evans, E. (2016). The Economics of Free: Freemium Games, Branding and the Impatience Economy. *Convergence: The International Journal of Research into New Media Technologies*, 22(6), 563–580.

Fisher, E. (2022). *Algorithms and Subjectivity: The Subversion of Critical Knowledge*. London: Routledge.

Gault, M. (2021, February 15). Billionaires See VR as a Way to Avoid Radical Social Change. *Wired*, https://www.wired.com/story/billionaires-use-vr-avoid-social-change.

Gekker, A. and Hind, S. (2020). Infrastructural Surveillance. *New Media & Society*, 22(8), 1414–1436.

Hamilton, K. A., Lee, S. Y., Chung, U. C., Liu, W., and Duff, B. R. (2021). Putting the 'Me' in Endorsement: Understanding and Conceptualizing Dimensions of Self-Endorsement Using Intelligent Personal Assistants. *New Media & Society*, 23(6), 1506–1526.

Hackl, C. (2020, July 5). The Metaverse is Coming and It's a Very Big Deal. *Forbes*, https://www.forbes.com/sites/cathyhackl/2020/07/05/the-metaverse-is-coming--its-a-very-big-deal/?sh=4df2bc2b440f.

Hao, K. and Swart, H. (2022, April 19). South Africa's Private Surveillance Machine Is Fuelling a Digital Apartheid. *MIT Technology Review*, https://www.technologyreview.com/2022/04/19/1049996/south-africa-ai-surveillance-digital-apartheid/.

Hepp, A. (2020). *Deep Mediatization*. London: Routledge.

Hepp, A., Hjarvard, S. and Lundby, K. (2015). Mediatization: Theorizing the Interplay between Media, Culture and Society. *Media, Culture & Society*, 37(2), 314–324.

Herian, R. (2021). *Data: New Trajectories in Law*. London: Routledge.

Hjarvard, S. (2008). The Mediatization of Society: A Theory of the Media as Agents of Social and Cultural Change. *Nordicom Review*, 29(2), 105–134.

Kaplan, M. (2019). The Digital Potlatch: The Uses of Uselessness in the Digital Economy. *New Media & Society*, 21(9), 1947–1966.

Krasmann, S. (2020). The Logic of the Surface: On the Epistemology of Algorithms in Times of Big Data. *Information, Communication & Society*, 23(14), 2096–2109.

Kukkakorpi, M. and Pantti, M. (2021). A Sense of Place: VR Journalism and Emotional Engagement. *Journalism Practice*, 15(6), 785–802.

Lemley, M. A. and Volokh, E. (2018). Virtual Reality and Augmented Reality. *University of Pennsylvania Law Review*, 66(5), 1051–1138.

Lupton, D. (2020a). Wearable Devices: Sociotechnical Imaginaries and Agential Capacities. In I. Pedersen and A. Iliadis (eds.) *Embodied Computing: Wearables, Implantables, Embeddables, Ingestibles* (pp. 49–69). Cambridge: The MIT Press.

Lupton, D. (2020b). *Data Selves*. Cambridge: Polity.

Lupton, D. (2020c). The Internet of Things: Social Dimensions. *Sociology Compass*, 14(4), 1–13.

Lury, C. and Wakeford, N. (2012). *Inventive Methods: The Happening of the Social*. London: Routledge.

Mabrook, R. (2021). Between Journalist Authorship and User Agency: Exploring the Concept of Objectivity in VR Journalism. *Journalism Studies*, 22(2), 209–224.

Mayer-Schönberger, V. and Ramge, T. (2019). *Reinventing Capitalism in the Age of Big Data*. London: John Murray.

Mosco, V. (2017). *Becoming Digital: Toward a Post-Internet Society*. Bingley: Emerald Publishing.

Nowotny, H. (2022). *In AI We Trust: Power, Illusion and Control of Predictive Algorithms*. Cambridge: Polity Press.

Oliver, T. (2020). *The Self Delusion: The Surprising Science of How We Are Connected and Why that Matters*. London: Weidenfeld & Nicolson.

Pedersen, I. and Iliadis, A. (2020). Embodied Computing. In I. Pedersen and A. Iliadis (eds.) *Embodied Computing: Wearables, Implantables, Embeddables, Ingestibles* (pp. ix–xxxix). Cambridge: The MIT Press.

Poell, T., Nieborg, D. and Duffy, B. E. (2022). *Platforms and Cultural Production*. Cambridge: Polity.

Rubin, P. (2020). *Future Presence: How Virtual Reality is Changing Human Connection, Intimacy, and the Limits of Ordinary Life*. New York: Harper One.

Sandvik, K. B. (2020). Wearables for Something Good: Aid, Dataveillance and the Production of Children's Digital Bodies. *Information, Communication & Society*, 23(14), 2014–2029.

Seubert, S. and Beckert, C. (2019). The Culture Industry Revisited: Sociophilosophical Reflections on 'Privacy' in the Digital Age. *Philosophy and Social Criticism*, 45(8), 930–947.

Siggelkow, N. and Terwiesch, C. (2019). *Connected Strategy: Building Continuous Customer Relationships for Competitive Advantage*. Boston: Harvard Business Review Press.

Srnicek, N. (2017). *Platform Capitalism*. Cambridge: Polity Press.

Stiegler, C. (2021). *The 360° Gaze: Immersions in Media, Society, and Culture*. Cambridge: The MIT Press.

Sundar, S. S. (2020). Rise of Machine Agency: A Framework for Studying the Psychology of Human-AI Interaction (HAII). *Journal of Computer-Mediated Communication*, 25, 74–88.

Syvertsen, T. (2020). *Digital Detox: The Politics of Disconnecting*. Bingley: Emerald Publishing.

The Onlife Initiative. (2015). The Onlife Manifesto. In L. Floridi (ed.) *The Onlife Manifesto: Being Human in a Hyperconnected Era* (pp. 7–13). Cham: Springer.

Tucker, I. (2018). Digitally Mediated Emotion: Simondon, Affectivity and Individuation. In T. D. Sampson, S. Maddison and D. Ellis (eds.) *Affect and Social Media: Emotion, Mediation, Anxiety and Contagion* (pp. 35–41). London and Lanham: Rowman & Littlefield.

Tulloch, R. and Johnson, C. (2022). Games and Data Capture Culture: Play in the Era of Accelerated Neoliberalism. *Media, Culture & Society*, 44(5), 922–934.

van Dijck, J. (2021). Seeing the Forest for the Trees: Visualizing Platformization and Its Governance. *New Media & Society*, 23(9), 2801–2819.

van Dijck, J., Poell, T. and de Waal, M. (2018). *The Platform Society: Public Values in a Connective World*. Oxford: Oxford University Press.

Velkova, J. and Kaun, A. (2019). Algorithmic Resistance: Media Practices and the Politics of Repair. *Information, Communication & Society*, doi: 10.1080/1369118X.2019.1657162.

Ytre-Arne, B. and Das, R. (2021). Audiences' Communicative Agency in a Datafied Age: Interpretative, Relational and Increasingly Prospective. *Communication Theory*, 31(4), 779–797.

Zuboff, S. (2019). *The Age of Surveillance Capitalism: The Fight for a Human Future at the New Frontier of Power*. London: Profile Books.

3 Understanding the Metaverse

Beyond the Hype

Technically, the metaverse is still a rather long way off. Nevertheless, the economic promises for platforms to effectively monopolise their users are clear, thus driving investment. Such promises, however, also mean competition, which will ultimately leave only a handful of dominant platforms that will function as whole-life interfaces for their users. For the latter, meanwhile, the metaverse would be a space to perform one's avatar and, therefore, identity in a virtual form. Effectively, this means the virtualisation of the social world. This world will be avatar-centric, leading to a co-constitution of the avatar and the human user. The necessity to build and present the virtual self and project a deliberate image through the avatar will, therefore, drive spending on avatar customisations, kickstarting a metaverse economy. Likewise, virtual goods and experiences will become more than just about passing time but will, instead, be constitutive of the self. Nevertheless, the immersiveness and data richness of the metaverse, combined with a foreseeable reliance on AI intermediaries, open the door for manipulation and disinformation. There are, of course, also less nefarious uses of the metaverse but, as the discussion of non-fungible tokens (NFTs) demonstrates, fundamental issues remain unresolved.

3.1 Building the Metaverse: Key Opportunities and Challenges

The origin story of the metaverse has to begin with games (see Ong 2021) – after all, these were the original immersive digital worlds; many of them, particularly the more recent ones, also have in-built economies – not the imaginary economies of some world-building games but, instead, ones straddling the online and the offline, in which e.g. digital items are traded between players for either in-game or conventional currency. However, the metaverse also represents a further qualitative step. Particularly, while games tend to offer only bounded virtual experience, the metaverse will

DOI: 10.4324/9781003355861-3

likely be (or, at least, feel) all-encompassing; this includes not only freedom of movement and action unconstrained by a game scenario but also a wide range of functionalities and experiences, ranging from work to leisure to interaction (Batchelor 2021). In that sense, nothing would, practically speaking, be outside the metaverse. Another likely difference is that, while game experiences are centrally designed, many, if not most, of the experiences across the metaverse are likely to be user-generated, leading to the emergence of new creator economies and social experiences (Radoff 2021a). *Roblox* is a notable example here: while it still consists of a multitude of centrally hosted gaming experiences within a unified platform, those are user-generated, leading to the emergence of a developer economy, although one in which platforms play a central role.

At the moment, though, the metaverse occupies a paradoxical position: on the one hand, there is a lot of talk on what it would look like and what commercial opportunities it would open up but, on the other hand, there still needs to be a major upgrade in the currently existing technology, and, where such technologies are already available, convenience and affordability remain an issue (Wiederhold 2022: 1). Hence, the metaverse is emerging as 'the outcome of the convergence of a range of nascent and extant digital and online technologies' (Murphy et al. 2021), even though a full convergence of this kind still lies in the future. One of the key tasks ahead is the improvement of the performance and wearability of VR technologies, such as headsets, so that they can be worn all or most of one's waking time (Clark 2021). Likewise, challenges lie ahead in terms of making the metaverse truly co-present, instead of spreading users across different servers, to make experiences truly non-bounded – something that is currently still beyond even the most advanced virtual games and other experiences (Batchelor 2021; Ball 2022). Current proto-metaverse experiences merely provide an illusion of simultaneity: even in massive virtual concerts attracting audiences of millions, users are split into batches that have identical content streamed to them (Koss 2020). Moreover, what still lies beyond even the most advanced gaming or virtual experiences of today is creating the mechanics of experience that does not rely on shortcuts but, instead, provides for full immersion, particularly in terms of simulated space and physics (Batchelor 2021). On the other hand, it transpires that, at least at a proto-metaverse level (and potentially beyond), having a broad enough set of bounded experiences (as in e.g. *Fortnite* or *Roblox*) is a successful strategy (and cartoonish graphics is not an issue either – think of *Roblox* or *Minecraft*).

In lieu of one-size-fits-all descriptions, three principles for metaverse design outlined by Hackl, Lueth and Di Bartolo (2022: 16) can be of use: these are experience, identity, and ownership. While it is reasonably certain that the metaverse will be premised on interactive, engaging, and user-centric experiences that will allow for the creation of a fully-fledged identity (that may or may not correspond to the offline self), the matter of ownership is far less certain. As will be argued later in the book, there currently are limited, if any, mechanisms for ascertaining ownership in the metaverse, while some of the currently touted solutions (e.g. tokens of various sorts) are more likely to be mere distractions or user retention techniques rather than truly useful tools. At best, there is a subjective *sense* of ownership, often as a matter of sunken costs (financial or labour, as in e.g. content generation).

Once realised, the metaverse is anticipated to lead to 'a seamless convergence of our physical and digital lives', enabling users to 'work, play, relax, transact and socialize' virtually (J. P. Morgan n.d.). Thereby, such an artificial environment could not only stand in for but also largely replace the quality of sensory immersion as well as social connection and interaction with others – in other words, '*social richness*', which can be defined as 'the awareness of being one actor among many in a social environment' (Bolter, Engberg and MacIntyre 2021: 75). Hence, the feasibility of the metaverse rests not only on technology but also on people, that is, their adoption, frequency and duration of use, and willingness to enter into virtual interactions. Of course, advances in AI would also enable simulation of human users; nevertheless, while there is an expectation that such automated avatars 'will enhance the experience for users, creating a desire to continue to engage with a virtual world' (Wiederhold 2022: 2), and, as argued below, it is likely that such automated avatars would play a prominent role in virtual sociality, the lack of *human* uptake would undermine the entire purpose of the metaverse and its datafication and monetisation strategy (there is little use in advertising to automated avatars).

To some, the metaverse hype might be more anticipatory than based on existing technology; nevertheless, even if that was likely the case, no technology company would take the risk of being left out once the technology arrives (Alvim 2022). As a fully always-on and on-demand metaverse would also necessitate improvements in connection technology, including going beyond full rollout of 5G into, potentially, 6G, the introduction of the metaverse to users would 'start off as a focus for gaming, virtual reality, digital meeting spaces, digital assets' before becoming fully all-encompassing, immersive, and completely social (Murphy et al. 2021). The enabling ingredients notwithstanding, the actual technology that brings the nuts and bolts together and one on which the metaverse will run is AI (Rosenberg 2022). It is only with an AI engine pulling the strings that the diverse elements making up virtual worlds can be both enabled and then brought together into a meaningful system, content generated and adapted seamlessly and surreptitiously, and virtual experiences moderated for unwanted content and behaviour. However, it is very easy to underappreciate the sheer amount of computational power and energy resources that would be necessary to simulate and moderate an all-encompassing dynamic experience for a very large number of concurrent users (Batchelor 2021). For this reason, the development of a fully all-encompassing metaverse would necessitate a further technological leap, likely associated with quantum computing.

While the necessary upfront investment will be significant, it is easy to understand why the metaverse is appealing to technology companies – it is all about grabbing users' attention as they engage with content inside the metaverse and separating them from the outside, i.e. from experience-unrelated stimuli (Bailenson 2018: 67; Ghaffary 2021). Moreover, the metaverse also involves the collection of more data than e.g. traditional social media, including gestures and movements, voice, gaze, etc. (Virgilio 2022). Unsurprisingly, if the struggle for the metaverse is a struggle for user attention (in terms of both data generation and content supply), then it must also be a struggle for platform dominance in order to become a universal, life-encompassing operating system that mediates and manages user interactions with the rest of the world (Ghaffary 2021; see also Vaidhyanathan 2018) and the data thus generated (Ahvenainen 2022). All this would have to be done at the expense of competing platform offerings.

In such a cutthroat environment, a multitude of competing metaverse platforms would not be able to thrive; instead, only those providing the most immersive, engaging, and tailored experiences would survive – as metaverse platforms become the interfaces for the whole life, users would be unlikely to switch but would, instead, invest in and stick with a platform of their choice. Hence, even if an open standard allowing for free migration across metaverse platforms is set (although, as Ball (2022) acknowledges, this would not be as easy as some metaverse enthusiasts allege), it is still likely that some experience providers would receive a larger share of attention while others would ultimately dwindle. After all, such a drive towards concentration and domination of several surviving players is typical of the platformisation logics across domains (Poell, Nieborg and Duffy 2022: 42). Indeed, the more time is spent and the more money (virtual or conventional) is invested – in short, the higher the sunken costs – the higher user engagement and loyalty will be (Eyal 2019: 10).

This competitive aspect underscores the reasoning why Bolter, Engberg and MacIntyre (2021: 138) describe the claim that the metaverse would be 'a single, transparent experience – a perfect, coherent, alternate world' as merely a myth. Instead, existing practice shows that, to capitalise on data pools that will be generated to create immersive metaverse experiences, platforms will have to be walled rather than integrated (Clark 2022).

Indeed, if anything can be learned from internet and computer technology history, it is that 'there is often room for only a limited number of platforms in any particular domain or activity' (McAffee and Brynjolfsson 2017: 168). Likewise, according to Faber (2022), it would be overly far-fetched to imagine that 'we will be able to navigate seamlessly through a series of connected virtual experiences' because that would necessitate a sudden change of long-standing business practices and harmonisation of multiple proprietary technologies. A more realistic version of the future would, therefore, be a metaverse composed of platforms, 'each controlled by a single company with its own slant and stable of branded properties' (Faber 2022), that is, the evolved platformisation scenario espoused in this book. Ultimately, then, the organisation of the metaverse would be recognisable vis-à-vis earlier and current versions of the digital in which a limited number of players dominate (Bolter, Engberg and MacIntyre 2021: 139).

There is an important distinction between platformisation and decentralisation. While platformisation has already been outlined, according to the decentralisation hypothesis, not only would the metaverse retain a plural character (that much is shared with platformisation, although decentralisation predictions typically also involve a high degree of interoperability) but also it would spread across a plethora of independent creators (individuals and companies), thus avoiding concentration of power, while governance functions would be largely carried out by the users themselves. In line with this promise, according to some current reports, decentralisation and focus on blockchain would be key to transition from Web 2.0 to Web 3.0 (see e.g. J. P. Morgan n.d.; see also Stackpole 2022). From the standpoint embraced in this book, as already stated previously, such predictions are somewhat reminiscent of the (as it has turned out) unfounded discourse surrounding the early internet, particularly as imagined by cyber libertarians. Here it is proposed that the distinguishing feature of Web 3.0 would be immersion (in 3D metaverse environments) rather than a specific mode of organisation and governance. This would also be in clear continuation of the development from static Web 1.0 to social and interactive Web 2.0 and now to immersive and all-encompassing Web 3.0, without prejudice to the way in which it is created and delivered to users.

Immersion also implies there being no need to leave a particular platform for any other competing service – or, for that matter, for the physical world. Indeed, as Bogost (2021) stresses, metaverse platforms would be characterised by 'total consolidation', whereby 'one entity sells you entertainment, social connection, trousers, antifreeze, and everything in between', integrating the entire stack from resources to consumer targeting and the actual sale, subsuming everything under a single service – 'the black hole of consumption'. With a limited number of such behemoths sharing (almost) the entire market, the metaverse might offer technology companies the opportunity for integration of their acquisition portfolios across diverse domains of life, capitalising on such integration to lock users in as much as possible: consolidation of assets as consolidation of power (D'Anastasio 2021a). For this reason, there are already calls for decentralisation and permissionless participation – for example, while in principle anyone can write a piece of software for a computer operating system, the situation is very different for gaming consoles or proto-metaverse platforms, such as *Roblox*, where owners have total and complete control; it is the latter scenario that such critics call out against (Radoff 2021b).

Likewise, should multiple metaverse platforms coexist, it is far from clear whether both technological gear and virtual avatars would be compatible across platforms (Morse and Stein 2022). In terms of hardware, one is likely to ultimately be able to access multiple platform options through a given headset; if there were going to be secluded device–platform ecosystems, there would likely be a limited number of them (think of Windows/ Android vs MacOS/iOS, PlayStation vs Xbox). This might be one of the tasks that the newly established Metaverse Standards Forum might be able to achieve. Once one is in, though, different platforms would likely retain their walled nature, just like e.g. one's Facebook profile is not automatically synchronised across Twitter, LinkedIn, TikTok, etc., except in cases when some of the smaller services may connect to larger ones, in a manner not dissimilar to currently signing in to non-Meta/Alphabet services using one's Facebook or Google account. Ultimately, as the key variable in any digital platform context is data about users, their interactions, and environments (Andrejevic 2020: 97), the drive to concentrate such extraction at the exclusion of any competitors would, likely, be too strong for openness and interoperability to be developed.

According to the early voices offering projections of the metaverse, of key importance would be the ability to express one's identity through customisable avatars that can hop between different environments and experiences, the ability to socialise with on- and offline friends, the ability to fully immerse oneself in the virtual world, the variety of interests and tastes that are accommodated within the virtual world, easy and frictionless transition between experiences, synchronicity of experience with human and non-human agents – all as an amalgamation of contributions by individuals, commercial actors, various organised groups, etc., benefitting from a fully functioning internal economy (Ball 2020; Kleeman 2021; Mantegna 2021). While such future projections are, again, overly optimistic on the matter of interoperability and there being a unified experience of the metaverse, what they capture is the centrality of seamless interactive experiences through avatars and a place for the self to be performed, with others, in a virtual form. Of course, the performance of the self is ever-present in any life situations, but it is taken to the next level in the metaverse. In other words, the metaverse is projected to be more than just social media on steroids – instead, it is foreseen as a virtual recreation of most of human social life and one that involves the convergence of all forms of media and entertainment in which technology companies have complete control over user behaviours, internal economies, etc. (Batchelor 2021).

In the above context, one should not be surprised by the fact that discussions of presence have also become more complex and demanding. Notably, the notion of presence has expanded from simply subjective perception of 'being there' (although this definition has not completely fallen out of use – see e.g. Han, Bergs and Moorhouse 2022: 7) to a combination of '(1) individual perception of the world and (2) social interaction and engagement with others' (Bolter, Engberg and MacIntyre 2021: 73). The social aspect is crucial here: interaction not only adds to the realism of the experience but also contributes to the sunken costs as the investment in building and maintaining relationships, the gravitational pull of existing social ties, and the experience of previous (and expectation of future) engagement only further contribute to locking users in. Hence, even outwardly less realistic environments (e.g. in terms of graphics) can be fully immersive if the content and interaction summands are capable of invoking sufficient cues for the brain to perceive it as 'real' (Wiederhold 2022: 2). Simultaneously, the visceral nature of virtual experiences (where one can see and sense what is happening, as opposed to simply imagining while reading a book) both allows for greater empathy through self-projection *and* constitutes a source of psychological harm when such projected self is placed in distressing situations (Mabrook 2021: 210).

Neither immersive worlds nor the ability to create personalised avatars are new as such; they have long been part and parcel of the video game industry, giving users recognisability of the phenomenon; the metaverse, however, should take the experience beyond the confines of a single game world and be multi-purpose (Alvim 2022). Likewise, compared with, for example, conventional video games, the metaverse opens up significantly deeper engagement opportunities that, in turn, allow for more effective (and likely surreptitious) audience attraction and retention, not least because of a stronger emotional response to content and the unfolding story (Pallavicini, Pepe and Minissi 2019: 152) – and content here needs to be understood not only in terms of the core experience but also as sponsored and other commercial content. After all, while the metaverse would necessitate and integrate a range of technological, content, and usage innovations, one thing is bound to remain a staple – advertising, or at least some form thereof (Taylor 2022: 383).

When generating virtual worlds and socialities, an even deeper level of influence by platform companies can be expected. Here one should see the opportunity (no doubt to be embraced by platform companies) to shape not only individuals, but also entire societies. After all, it is futile to imagine the individual and the society as separate entities – instead, they are 'fundamentally entangled with each other', whereby '[t]he various institutions that make up society only exist in and through the social practices of individuals' while, reciprocally, 'the individual only exists in the light of the social relations in which he or she engages' (Hepp 2020: 102). Crucially, then, with technologies ever more deeply intermediating the interaction between individuals and their societies (Hepp 2020: 102–103), the shaping of life and experience (something the metaverse platforms would surely be capable of), particularly when extended across a substantial number of individuals, would correspondingly affect how societies unfold. One should also add a third interrelated element – technology that significantly affects both how individuals shape society and how they understand and interact with that society (Annany 2016: 100; see also Kalpokas 2021). However, technology typically remains proprietary to the companies themselves. Hence, while there is already significant debate about the effects of platforms on social and political processes, with the advent of the metaverse, such shaping power of platforms would become even more all-encompassing.

Crucially, social interactions do not refer solely to human users and their avatars but also to the avatars of automated characters – bots – that would likely frequent the metaverse. Sometimes they could be deceptive, as many (but not all) current social media bots are, and sometimes they may be ancillary, as non-player characters in video games are. Nevertheless, they would enter into social interactions of one kind or another, impacting upon individuals and, through them, the entire social stratum, further deepening the idea of a tripartite – human, technological, and societal – interaction. In terms of realism and interaction quality, though, some early indications could be drawn from research on the early-stage precursors of such automated avatars: chatbots. If an artificial entity is capable of evoking a sense of it having an independent 'mind' of sorts (i.e., not behaving in accordance with strictly prescribed patterns), and if the language used can be perceived as expressive of emotional states and suggestive of active listening, research shows that humans can be drawn into quasi-social relationships (Lee, Lee and Sah 2021: 936). It is worth noting that the threshold is not extremely high: it is all about *perception* of mind and emotion rather than their true presence – the social role of artificial entities is in the eye of the beholder.

Here it must be kept in mind that imagination and interpretation are paramount when constructing a sense of the self and of the world: as Charter (2019: 4) puts it, '[w]e invent interpretations of ourselves and other people in the flow of experience, just as we conjure up interpretations of fictional characters from a flow of written text'. Emphasis here is on the malleability and adaptability of the human mind whereby any change in circumstances (such as a move from physical to digital environments or encounters with diverse – human and artificial – actors) is simply thought into a permanently evolving representation of the world. In that sense, humans' access to themselves and the world around them is simply based on reading, interpreting, and projecting meaning into the states and behaviours of the self and of others – reality as such then becomes a matter of perception, understanding, and interpretation, a phenomenon of the mind, a meaning and a story cobbled together from disparate pieces of sensory information (Charter 2019: 7, 189–190). Hence, building a world of controlled (or algorithmically moderated) sensory information, particularly one that would be a one-stop-shop for most, if not all, of the senses, would effectively mean 'hacking' the human consciousness (for the neuroscientific preconditions of such hacking, see e.g. Charter 2019: 141–144). Again, the amount of power over individual identities and societal processes and the capacity to shape them in accordance with any vested interests, held by platform companies, would be very significant indeed.

Here, the immersive nature of the metaverse once again is at the heart of the matter: it is notable that even textual cues have been demonstrated to create 'electronic elsewheres', namely, 'social spaces sustained through digitally enabled affective structures' (Papacharissi 2015: 24), and, thus, being more all-encompassing (and built on stronger visual and, in the near future, tactile cues), the metaverse would sustain experiences linked to highly impactful and long-lasting 'electronic elsewheres'. No less importantly, a new form of temporality is created, one that had already been evident on social media and will only be strengthened by the metaverse – 'a temporality that is concerned with "the now", and is stretched and condensed in various ways' (Coleman 2018: 68). In other words, it is all about what is happening currently, what can be shared and experienced together, jumping over what is not representable (or not represented) straight towards another experience (stretching) and converging upon what is trending (condensing). Once again, this represents substantial opportunities for metaverse platforms to make use of their experience architecture and content moderation to shape the very way life is lived and, following the platform competition imperative, to lock individuals within their walled gardens ever more effectively.

3.2 Experiencing the Metaverse: Enhancements and Limitations

Gaming, working, studying, enjoying brand experiences, attending virtual parties and concerts, creating art, or simply hanging out – these and any other conceivable activities would be supported by the underlying infrastructure and code, allegedly allowing people to travel between different worlds, taking their identities wherever they go (Koss 2020; Wakefield 2021). Again, while for most metaverse enthusiasts such world-hopping would be of a cross-platform kind, this book presents the case that it would only be platform-internal. For most ordinary users of the metaverse, though, this might be a very abstract issue. After all, the truly important bit is that users *feel* like they are getting a broad enough scope of a 'multi-world' experience that caters to them. Hence, even having the opportunity to use the same avatar across multiple experiences and games on the same platform would make 'thousands of disparate games feel like part of the same universe' (Parkin 2022). For this reason, there would probably be limited user pressure for greater interoperability and horizontal integration – just like today, it would be difficult to find calls for greater integration and interoperability between, say, TikTok, LinkedIn, and Tinder.

It is crucial to keep in mind that '[t]he metaverse is about identity in ways that haven't been possible before' (Hackl 2020), namely, taking the permanently malleable digital life already lived in the digital environment (see Kalpokas 2021) even further. Particularly given the virtual nature of the metaverse, it is personal storytelling and self-expression that really matter in the avatar-mediated virtual interactions (Barry 2021). Effectively, the avatar becomes the carrier of information that the user intends to deliver to others – and several generations have already grown accustomed to their digital identities (albeit significantly more limited ones) being a crucial part of who they are (Hackl, Lueth and Di Bartolo 2022: 110–111). On the flip side, the pressures inherent in building one's online persona have become familiar as well. No less importantly, the avatar expresses not only identity but also belonging (demonstration of allegiance to a tribe) and status (signalling one's position to others), thereby implying more user work on their avatars and more commercial opportunities for brands to offer community- and status-signifying goods (Terry and Keeley 2022: 122).

Crucially, it transpires that the avatar and the actual human person become locked in a dialectic relationship with one another, implying a direct mutual effect (Procter 2021). Moreover, creation of virtual avatars would also potentially enable greater playfulness and flexibility in trying out and combining multiple identities, often such that the users cannot express in their offline lives (Scholz and Duffy 2018: 14). Simultaneously, though, the effect does not extend one way (from user to avatar). A notable phenomenon to be kept in mind here is the so-called 'proteus effect', denoting identification with one's own avatar, mentally assuming its qualities and characteristics but also perceiving others' attitudes towards one's avatar as those towards oneself (Fox, Bailenson and Tricase 2013). In an important way, therefore, the individual '*becomes* the avatar, eradicating any separate distinction between the physical self and the re-embodied self' (Scholz and Duffy 2018: 14). Hence, one could think of the person and the avatar as involved in a relationship of co-constitution.

Consequently, virtual items that help customise either one's avatar or virtual premises associated with that avatar (e.g. virtual dwellings) are not just constitutive of self-expression and self-presentation but also have been demonstrated to give rise to a sense of ownership on par with that caused by possessing physical items (Carozzi et al. 2019). Meanwhile, brand forays into the metaverse represent 'a new era of virtual–real world interplay, a space in which smart product placement meets the desire of consumers to express their personalities in the virtual world' (Barry 2021). In fact, it transpires that, for the digital natives, virtual goods can be more valuable than the tangible ones are, simply owing to the former's visibility and frequency of use (Barry 2021). A similar observation is also in order with regard to avatar customisation – regardless of whether the avatar itself is a digital recreation of the user themselves or a fantasy one. The necessity to ramp up one's self-presentation is already evident in traditional social media, e.g. in the form of AR face filters that have turned from a gimmick to a staple. While the ease, flexibility, and fluidity of both appearance and identity, combined with the playfulness inherent in the ability to manipulate one's appearance, can, in some cases at least, be seen as a liberating experience, this new kind of self-representation also implies additional pressures with regard to compliance with virtual beauty standards. Even if this pivot towards the avatar decreases the pressure on one's physical appearance (although there is no guarantee – in fact, there could be an additional pressure to match a virtual appearance), an increase of pressure to spend money on avatar customisations can be foreseen.

Such self-expressive function would, however, extend beyond the avatar into the content domain as well. After all, already in today's social media, content generated and/or shared by the user serves as a crucial identity and reputation-building tool. As Kleeman (2021) stresses, '[m]ore than in most games and online experiences that preceded this, metaverse users will build and shape the space they use', if not in terms of governance (the favourite claim of decentralisation advocates), then in terms of the actual experience. Unlike the physical world, where there is bodily presence and a long-standing track record to be relied upon, the metaverse represents a self-assembly world and identity (although not completely do-it-yourself owing to the inherent architectural limitations and readily provided building blocks that are part and parcel of platforms). Unsurprisingly, therefore, 'creation will be as much a part of the experience as consumption' (Kleeman 2021). *Roblox* is a good example here, providing an easy-to-use toolkit for anyone to create game worlds within the platform that other users are then able to explore and play (Wakefield 2021).

Nevertheless, there does seem to be potential for abuse in these digital environments, particularly when content generation and governance are not linked, with *Roblox* again being a noteworthy example. In terms of its modus operandi, *Roblox* is a user-generated content platform par excellence – it allows users to create their own games and experiences and play each other's creations, with the visit count for the most popular ones measuring in the billions; what is no less important – creators get remunerated as a fraction of the revenue generated by their game or experience (D'Anastasio 2021b). However, the latter happens at a rate that can be seen as extortionate: while traditional game stores would hand around 70% of the revenue to the developers, in *Roblox* it is just 25%; moreover, there are also penalties for cashing out: creators are remunerated with the in-game currency, robux, and converting it to traditional currency leaves one with just around a third of what it would cost to purchase the same amount of robux (D'Anastasio 2021b). Hence, the platform can be seen as reaping most of the benefit while also locking users inside the platform's economy by disincentivising cashing out. Of course, a counter-argument could be that, unlike traditional game stores, *Roblox* is providing developers with access not just to players but also to the entire toolkit and ecosystem; moreover, the very fact that creators *are* remunerated is not unimportant: for example, social media platforms are completely reliant on user-generated content, and yet their business models are premised on entirely free user labour. Nevertheless, as the metaverse develops into a fully-fledged virtual economy, the fairness and regulatability of business practices will become matters of pressing concern. For the time being, at least, there is strong business sense in the above practices: when virtual worlds make their own in-game currency difficult or expensive to cash out, users are encouraged to spend any in-game earnings on in-game items (e.g. to customise one's avatar), thereby stimulating the in-game economy (Koss 2020) while also providing an additional disincentive to leave for a competing platform.

Still, as repeatedly stressed throughout this book, mere content would not be enough – what truly matters is virtual socialising. Indeed, socialising has been a significant driver behind the rise in popularity of proto-metaverse platforms, such as *Roblox* or *Fortnite*, and, while the pandemic has, of course, played a crucial role here, metaverse enthusiasts expect the trend to continue post-COVID as well (Wakefield 2021). Similarly, the expectation is that, by becoming the norm, virtual events attracting massive audiences will 'push the boundaries of interactivity, changing the nature of live experiences' (Wakefield 2021). The scale of such events will make the sale of virtual tickets and merchandise very profitable indeed (Howcroft 2021), including new themed experiences for artists to engage with audiences and thus generate value through in-game activities, virtual concerts, or virtual merchandise. In this way, shared experiences of content consumption or fandom more broadly are made possible without partaking in a shared space and on a scale larger than any shared physical space could accommodate (Perez 2021). This, of course, also involves a major cultural and perceptual shift – after all, in the conventional understanding, neither such events nor merchandise are 'real' (Pryor 2021). In addition to massive events, such as concerts, a further summand of note would be shared consumption of video content, be it TV or streaming; whether the central organisational unit of such consumption would be a channel that aggregates intellectual property (more akin to today's television or streaming) or single-brand experiences (e.g. *Star Wars*-only), remains to be seen (Kleeman 2021). Nevertheless, this would be the basis for collective enjoyment and identity-building through partaking in communities of consumption.

Simultaneously, the metaverse also provides brands with a valuable opportunity for creating their own virtual ecosystems and digital experiences that provide immersion and allow for increased relatability (Holmes 2021). With changing consumer behaviour, brands are increasingly pushed into virtual spaces that go beyond traditional Web presence, 'seeking to create digital doppelgangers of the goods and services they provide in the tangible world' (Mantegna 2021). Indeed, it is widely agreed that '[c]ompanies will need to transition their marketing strategies from online ad buys to existing in a shared, virtual economy' (Hackl 2020), but not only that: the vast and all-encompassing nature of the metaverse will likely usher in novel and complex digital assistants (far surpassing their current incarnations such as Siri) as gatekeepers and experience managers for human users. Hence, business considerations will additionally have to include 'the layer of business to robot to consumer, where virtual assistants and robots own the relationship with the consumer' (Hackl and Buzzell 2021: 207; for more on the gatekeeping function of digital assistants, see e.g. Mayer-Schönberger and Ramge 2019). Moreover, relationship building will also have to take account of social ties and influences that users will be able to form in the metaverse – and these relationships will involve not just other humans but also AI-enabled fully digital agents and other virtual actors (Hackl 2020).

Thinking of metaverse content more broadly, there is one more potential challenge that is only partly understood and often glossed over: that of manipulation. Metaverse users will take part in it for extended periods of time, meaning that the companies that are either curating the metaverse itself (in terms of the underlying hardware and code, i.e. the technology and platform companies) or providing particular experiences will be able to continuously monitor behaviour, responses to stimuli, and other kinds of data, enabling targeting with unprecedented precision (Murphy et al. 2021; see also Greengard 2019: 183; Tremayne and Gill 2021). In addition, manipulation-specific AI avatars, combined with data analytics capacities, could be employed for social engineering purposes, tricking users into suboptimal decisions (Falchuk, Loeb and Neff 2018: 54). Moreover, owing to the psychological impact of virtual experiences – a *feeling* of the experience being real, significantly more intensely than in the case of a screen – the believability of manipulative content would increase even further (Bailenson 2018: 67). Hence, one of the paramount dangers of the metaverse is 'not just that we are known, but that we can be led' (Tremayne and Gill 2021), rendering individual agency problematic.

Building on the above capacities, disinformation will be taken to a completely new level through the use of '[a]utomated, cross-reality illusions, tailor-made by using intimate knowledge of each individual's life and mental states' (Tremayne and Gill 2021). Hence, the entire perceptive and cognitive apparatus can be effectively 'hacked' (Mazarr et al. 2019). Given the effectiveness of manipulation on today's social media, which are significantly less immersive and data-rich than the metaverse will be, the potential for abuse is extremely worrying, meaning that new forms of (self-)regulation, media literacy, etc. will be necessary to tackle such threats. Particularly with the datafication capacities of the metaverse in mind, once such knowledge of the audiences becomes available to threat actors, resisting and combating tailored and targeted disinformation will become a particularly difficult task. In addition, just like in the current Web, content could be misinformative not out of a primary aim to mislead but simply with the purpose of commercial gain by catering to the biases and false assumptions that individuals have. There is no reason to believe that the metaverse would be any different.

Nevertheless, again like in the current economy, most money-making opportunities in the metaverse are less dubious. Still, in order to make the economic shift from physical to virtual viable, particularly in terms of content items and to further incentivise user activity, two elements are needed: items must be desirable and scarce. In terms of the latter, ownership is usually a way to make items scarce by precluding non-owners from making use of them. However, as argued below, ownership in the metaverse is a thorny issue. In many cases, though, even the *perception* of scarcity might be enough to increase desirability. It is on this perceptive level that NFTs or similar technologies may contribute to artificial scarcity by giving a digital object the clout (but not necessarily the reality) of being *the* original.

Here, one first needs to understand the difference between exchangeable (fungible) and non-exchangeable (non-fungible) tokens. Currencies, for example, are fungible because any note or coin can be exchanged for another of the same value, or one currency can be exchanged for another. That applies to cryptocurrencies as well (e.g. one bitcoin can be exchanged for another bitcoin). Consumer goods, food, etc. are also, for the most part, fungible as they can be exchanged for a set amount of currency (e.g. any bottle of milk of the same type and brand will be sold by a retailer for the same price, and it does not matter which bottle is picked from the shelf; so would be a chair or a TV). There are items, however, that cannot be so easily exchanged: paintings, diamonds, and other unique items that are always one of a kind cannot be easily exchanged one for another, just like a universal price cannot be set for all (or a specific subset) of them. Hence, they are non-exchangeable or non-fungible (see e.g. Fortnow and Terry 2022: 13). In the same manner, each NFT is created (minted) individually in relation to a particular digital object and, therefore, is one of a kind – an individual blockchain entry (Mendis 2021; Fortnow and Terry 2022). Notably, it could be observed that the adoption and use value of NFTs lies in their universality as '[a]ny digital work, including physical goods, which can be represented in a digital form, such as a photo, video or a scan' among a nearly limitless array of other things can be associated with an NFT (Guadamuz 2021). Nevertheless, as per below, the actual relationship between an NFT and an ostensibly represented good is a complicated one.

NFTs are beginning to show promise as the underpinning of the metaverse economy, not least because marketplaces are being set up for users to resell and exchange purchased NFTs or earn money by selling ones earned in-game (Jackson 2021). The universalisation of such marketplaces (their acceptance of NFTs from across different platforms) could be seen as an early step towards at least some functional interoperability between platforms, although that still does not mean that an NFT proof of 'ownership' of real estate in *Sandbox* would work in *Decentraland* or that one's avatar could stroll the latter adorned with an NFT-associated skin from *Roblox* – only that one can buy and sell them in different places. Matters get particularly complicated if there is, say, third-party intellectual property involved (say, an Avengers or Premier League-themed skin or a virtual designer handbag) that has been licensed to a particular metaverse platform on which the item had been purchased but not to the one to which the user intends to carry it.

It is easy to think that, through the use of NFTs, '[t]he change of ownership is recorded on the public blockchain to ensure there is no doubt over who owns what' (Winters 2021: 40; see also e.g. Hackl, Lueth and Di Bartolo 2022: 156–157) or that a new era in which a user owns all aspects of their online lives would be ushered in (see e.g. Terry and Keeney 2022: 23–24). Nevertheless, it must be stressed that, while it is clear who owns (and has owned in the past) which NFTs (because such records exist in a blockchain), it is by no means clear what that ownership actually *entails* – and it likely does not extend beyond the token itself (Moringiello and Odinet 2022). Still, for the more optimistically minded, NFTs continue to be seen as crucial to the interoperability of the metaverse: by providing a record of ownership (and a record of the terms and conditions of that ownership) that is recognised across platforms, they would, allegedly, allow users to exercise their property rights across the metaverse (Chayka 2021). However, it is crucial not to get overly excited, because such bold assertions often gloss over the question of what NFTs actually are. As Guadamuz (2021) pinpoints, 'non-fungible tokens are a metadata file that has been encoded using a work that may or may not be subject to copyright protection [...] or it could even be a work in the public domain' or it might already be a copy of an object, thus further undermining the idea of owning 'the original'. It should, then, come as no surprise that NFTs have attracted quite some controversy early on, such as famous masterpieces being put supposedly 'for sale' as NFTs, as in e.g. someone claiming to have certified their rights to the *Mona Lisa* by minting an NFT of a picture of the painting taken from a website (see e.g. ICO Examiner 2018). To take such claims seriously, though, is to completely misunderstand NFTs – whatever claim they have made would not be to the painting but to the digital picture – and even then, only to that single copy of that picture that they had saved on their device and used to mint the NFT in question.

However, the problem itself is real, as NFTs of items that are in the public domain or otherwise not owned by the seller of the NFT can be sold for high prices – and the onus is, effectively, on the buyer to ensure they are acquiring the 'real deal'. In fact, at the moment, the minters and sellers of NFTs can get away with virtually anything. For example, even minting and selling NFTs of works that still are protected by copyright (owned by someone else) is, most possibly, not illegal – at least because an NFT is neither a reproduction nor an adaptation (Guadamuz 2021). The latter could only encourage bogus actors to profit from NFTs that are, to all effect, worthless. In short, then, NFTs should be seen as content-agnostic, leading to the conclusion that 'in principle, NFTs have very little to do with copyright' (Guadamuz 2021). Even if there *are* rights to be transferred, purchasing an NFT certainly does not confer ownership of the object in question and of all the accompanying rights as well; instead, the actual thing that is acquired and owned is simply the metadata associated with the digital file – that is, the NFT narrowly conceived (Guadamuz 2021).

Against attempts to frame NFTs as somehow conferring indelible and otherwise objective ownership of an item (see e.g. Hackl and Buzzell 2021: 121), it must be stressed that '[c]reating an NFT of another thing – whether tangible or intangible – creates no legal link' (Moringiello and Odinet 2022:

36). Similarly, as Fortnow and Terry (2022: 219–220) stress, even in cases when NFTs associated with a copyrighted object are sold by the legitimate holder of that copyright, purchasing an NFT does not involve purchasing copyright – it remains with the creator (unless explicitly stipulated otherwise); this also has implications for what one can do with the acquired NFT: that typically involves personal (but not commercial) display, no right to make copies for sale, and no creation of derivatives (Fortnow and Terry 2022: 219–220). For this reason, any talk of digital theft in cases when an NFT is minted without the permission of the owner or creator of the underlying item (see e.g. Hackl and Buzzell 2021: 125) simply does not make sense. Some of those challenges could be solved if NFTs were framed (and minted) as a smart contract licensing certain uses of the object; the problem, nevertheless, is that this is typically not being done (Guadamuz 2021).

The property aspect of NFTs is further undermined as platforms reserve the right to deny access to purchased NFTs or to shut down a user's account altogether (Rizzo 2022). Indeed, it is the case that 'all visual and functional aspects of digital assets – the very features that give them any value – are not on the blockchain at all' but, instead, reside on the specific platforms and are, therefore, completely subjected to their terms and conditions, changes in business models, and managerial decisions – and unilaterally so (Marinotti 2022). Crucially, such items can be modified or even deleted – one would still own the NFT, but the object would be delinked from the blockchain entry; hence, instead of there being a bond of ownership, 'the platforms merely grant you access to the digital assets and only for the length of time they want' (Marinotti 2022). The situation may be different when transactions take place between persons where, upon the purchase of an NFT, the digital file is transferred to the buyer, although even then the intermediating platform retains significant rights, again including that of delinking (Marinotti 2022). Still, as the metaverse grows in scope and adoption, such private transactions would become increasingly niche anyway, sidelined by platform marketplaces.

This is not to say that NFTs cannot serve a useful function – for example, they can help assure provenance (chain of ownership) without the costly involvement of experts, thus contributing to solving a complex and expensive problem that has long plagued the art and collectables world (Fortnow and Terry 2022: 61–62). Also, while NFTs cannot be seen as capable of creating *actual* scarcity of virtual goods, they can, nevertheless, contribute to a *perception* of it and of there being an 'original'. The problem with such perception is that there is rarely any guarantee of a competing 'original' not being minted, particularly since the nature of rights transferred (if any) remains unclear. Ultimately, it all boils down to the matter of trust. Moreover, while the removal of third parties (dealers, auction houses, or other intermediaries) is often touted as decentralising the process and making it more expedient (see e.g. Fortnow and Terry 2022: 83), in practice this only contributes to the rise of new gatekeepers, such as NFT trading platforms (e.g. *OpenSea*). Where NFTs do hold promise, though, is in serving as an access key to exclusive experiences – a good example here would be owning a Bored Ape Yacht Club NFT and coextensively having access to their dedicated metaverse platform.

Additionally, NFTs have also been touted as serving a governance function, whereby token holders could vote on decisions affecting the platform community (J. P. Morgan n.d.). This is already the case on so-called decentralised apps as well as several proto-metaverse platforms where owners of virtual real estate can vote on governance matters. Nevertheless, while that sounds empowering and democratic on the surface (and definitely stands in stark contrast to the current one-sided decision-making of online platforms), it is only a partial democracy at best owing to its application of a property owners' census for making decisions that would affect not only their peers but also the vast majority of platform users who would only be frequenting such virtual premises without real opportunity of becoming members of the ruling class (a more extensive discussion of the matter is provided later in this book). Moreover, there is a further side effect – and one that is largely under-discussed. As governance functions, as well as property rights (inasmuch as they can be secured through NFTs), necessitate the owner to be identifiable, this not only undermines anonymity, often associated with fungible crypto assets, but it could also lead to significant privacy threats. By being identifiable by definition, NFTs create a public and indelible record identifying a wallet with an owner – and the more different elements of personal life are added to the blockchain (e.g. health records), the more pertinent the privacy threat becomes (Ravenscraft 2022; see also Edelman 2022). In short, then, little is straightforward about the metaverse and the building blocks thereof.

Bibliography

Ahvenainen, J. (2022, January 28). Metaverses Are Coming, but Who Owns Your Avatar? *Medium*, https://medium.com/prifina/metaverses-are-coming-but-who-owns-your-avatar-61ae9750f9c2.

Alvim, L. (2022, January 28). How the Metaverse Could Impact the World and the Future of Technology. *ABC News*, https://abcnews.go.com/Technology/metaverse-impact-world-future-technology/story?id=82519587.

Andrejevic, M. (2020). *Automated Media*. London: Routledge.

Annany, M. (2016). Toward an Ethics of Algorithms: Convening, Observation, Probability, and Timeliness. *Science, Technology & Human Values*, 41(1), 93–117.

Bailenson, J. (2018). *Experience on Demand: What Virtual Reality Is, How It Works, and What It Can Do*. New York: W. W. Norton and Company.

Ball, M. (2020). The Metaverse: Where to Find It, Who Will Build It, and Fortnite, https://www.matthewball.vc/all/themetaverse.

Ball, M. (2022). *The Metaverse and How It will Revolutionize Everything*. New York: Liveright Publishing Corporation.

Barry, C. (2021, June 9). Gucci Digitally Outfits Gen-Z in Metaverse Foray with *Roblox*. *AP News*, https://apnews.com/article/gucci-roblox-76339d10f139e9b0d39761bd8426c11e.

Batchelor, J. (2021, August 20). What Is the Metaverse, and Why Is It Worth so Much Money? *Games Industry*, https://www.gamesindustry.biz/articles/2021-08-20-what-is-the-metaverse-and-why-is-it-worth-so-much-money.

Bogost, I. (2021, October 28). The Metaverse Is Bad. *The Atlantic*, https://www.theatlantic.com/technology/archive/2021/10/facebook-metaverse-name-change/620449/.

Bolter, J. D., Engberg, M. and MacIntyre, B. (2021). *Reality Media: Augmented and Virtual Reality*. Cambridge: The MIT Press.

Carrozzi, A., Chylinski, M., Heller, J., Hilken, T., Keeling, D. I. and de Ruyter, K. (2019). What's Mine is a Hologram? How Shared Augmented Reality Augments Psychological Ownership. *Journal of Interactive Marketing*, 48, 71–88.

Charter, N. (2019). *The Mind Is Flat: The Illusion of Mental Depth and the Improvised Mind*. New Haven: Yale University Press.

Chayka, K. (2021, August 5). Facebook Wants Us to Live in the Metaverse. *The New Yorker*, https://www.newyorker.com/culture/infinite-scroll/facebook-wants-us-to-live-in-the-metaverse.

Clark, K. (2021, June 24). AR, the Metaverse and Why Marketers Need to be Thinking about the New 'Spatial' Web. *The Drum*, https://www.thedrum.com/news/2021/06/24/ar-the-metaverse-and-why-marketers-need-be-thinking-about-the-new-spatial-web.

Clark, K. (2022, January 20). The Metaverse Data Privacy Debate Is Getting Feisty: Here's what You Need to Know. *The Drum*, https://www.thedrum.com/news/2022/01/20/the-metaverse-data-privacy-debate-getting-feisty-here-s-what-you-need-know.

Coleman, R. (2018). Social Media and the Materialisation of the Affective Present. In T. D. Sampson, S. Maddison and D. Ellis (eds.) *Affect and Social Media: Emotion, Mediation, Anxiety and Contagion* (pp. 67–75). London: Rowman & Littlefield.

D'Anastasio, C. (2021a, November 4). The Metaverse Is Simply Big Tech, but Bigger. *Wired*, https://www.wired.com/story/big-tech-metaverse-internet-consolidation-business/.

D'Anastasio, C. (2021b, August 19). On *Roblox*, Kids Learn It's Hard to Earn Money Making Games. *Wired*, https://www.wired.com/story/on-roblox-kids-learn-its-hard-to-earn-money-making-games/.

Edelman, E. (2022, March 28). The Future of Digital Cash Is Not on the Blockchain. *Wired*, https://www.wired.com/story/digital-cash-ecash-act/.

Eyal, N. (2019). *Hooked: How to Build Habit-Forming Products*. London: Penguin.

Faber, T. (2022, March 8). Why Gamers are Sceptical of Zuckerberg's Metaverse. *Financial Times*, https://www.ft.com/content/0c0e45dc-b0df-4a1a-8dd0-70668ce64a99.

Falchuk, B., Loeb, S. and Neff, R. (2018). The Social Metaverse: Battle for Privacy. *IEEE Technology and Society Magazine*, 37(2), 52–61.

Fortnow, M. and Terry, Q. (2022). *The NFT Handbook: How to Create, Sell and Buy Non-Fungible Tokens*. Hoboken: Wiley.

Fox, J., Bailenson, J. N. and Tricase, L. (2013). The Embodiment of Sexualized Virtual Selves: The Proteus Effect and Experiences of Self-Objectification via Avatars. *Computers in Human Behavior*, 29, 930–938.

Ghaffary, S. (2021, November 24). Why You Should Care about Facebook's Big Push into the Metaverse. *Vox*, https://www.vox.com/recode/22799665/facebook-metaverse-meta-zuckerberg-oculus-vr-ar.

Greengard, S. (2019). *Virtual Reality*. Cambridge: The MIT Press.

Guadamuz, A. (2021, December). Non-Fungible Tokens (NFTs) and Copyright. *WIPO Magazine*, https://www.wipo.int/wipo_magazine/en/2021/04/article_0007.html.

Hackl, C. (2020, July 5). The Metaverse is Coming and It's a Very Big Deal. *Forbes*, https://www.forbes.com/sites/cathyhackl/2020/07/05/the-metaverse-is-coming--its-a-very-big-deal/?sh=4df2bc2b440f.

Hackl, C. and Buzzell, J. (2021). *The Augmented Workforce* (2nd ed.). North Kansas City: Renown Publishing.

Hackl, C., Lueth, D. and Di Bartolo, T. (2022). *Navigating the Metaverse: A Guide to Limitless Possibilities in a Web 3.0 World*. Hoboken: Wiley.

Han, D. D., Bergs, Y. and Moorhouse, N. (2022). Virtual Reality Consumer Experience Escapes: Preparing for the Metaverse. *Virtual Reality*, doi: 10.1007/s10055-022-00641-7.

Hepp, A. (2020). *Deep Mediatization*. London: Routledge.

Holmes, A. (2021, June 24). It's Time for Brands to Embrace the Metaverse. *Campaign Live*, https://www.campaignlive.co.uk/article/its-time-brands-embrace-metaverse/1720171.

Howcroft, E. (2021, April 19). The 'Metaverse' Bet: Crypto-Rich Investors Snap Up Virtual Real Estate. *Reuters*, https://www.reuters.com/business/metaverse-bet-crypto-rich-investors-snap-up-virtual-real-estate-2021-04-19/.

ICO Examiner. (2018, June 15). The Man Who Used the Blockchain to Steal the Mona Lisa, https://icoexaminer.com/ico-news/the-man-who-used-the-blockchain-to-lay-claim-to-the-mona-lisa/.

J. P. Morgan. (n.d.). Opportunities in the Metaverse: How Businesses Can Explore the Metaverse and Navigate the Hype vs Reality, https://www.jpmorgan.com/content/dam/jpm/treasury-services/documents/opportunities-in-the-metaverse.pdf.

Jackson, R. (2021, August 25). NFTs Are Here to Stay, Dominate and Slay. *Crunchbase*, https://news.crunchbase.com/news/nft-outlook-2021/.

Kalpokas, I. (2021). *Malleable, Digital, and Posthuman: A Permanently Beta Life*. Bingley: Emerald.

Kleeman, D. (2021, June 3). Kids Have Kickstarted the Metaverse. *Techonomy*, https://techonomy.com/2021/06/kids-have-kickstarted-the-metaverse/.

Koss, H. (2020, July 21). Are You Ready for the Metaverse? *Built In*, https://builtin.com/media-gaming/what-is-metaverse.

Lee, S., Lee, N. and Sah, Y. J. (2021). Perceiving a Mind in a Chatbot: Effect of Mind Perception and Social Cues on Co-Presence, Closeness, and Intention to Use. *International Journal on Human-Computer Interaction*, 36(1), 930–940.

Lewis, L., Owen, J., Fraser, H. and Digher, R. (2021, June). Non-Fungible Tokens (NFTs) and Copyright Law. *Bird & Bird*, https://www.twobirds.com/en/news/articles/2021/australia/non-fungible-tokens-nfts-and-copyright-law.

Mabrook, R. (2021). Between Journalist Authorship and User Agency: Exploring the Concept of Objectivity in VR Journalism. *Journalism Studies*, 22(2), 209–224.

Mantegna, M. (2021, June 10). The Metaverse: A Brave, New (Virtual) World. *Medium*, https://medium.com/berkman-klein-center/the-metaverse-a-brave-new-virtual-world-2f040cbae7d4.

Marinotti, J. (2022, May 3). Owning a Piece of the Metaverse Is Harder than you Think. *Slate*, https://slate.com/technology/2022/05/nfts-metaverse-property-ownership-not-so-fast.html.

Mayer-Schönberger, V. and Ramge, T. (2019). *Reinventing Capitalism in the Age of Big Data*. London: John Murray.

Mazarr, M. J., Bauer, R., Casey, A. Heintz, S. and Matthews, L. J. (2019). *The Emerging Risk of Virtual Societal Warfare: Social Manipulation in a Changing Information Environment*. Santa Monica: The RAND Corporation.

McAffee, A. and Brynjolfsson, E. (2017). *Machine, Platform, Crowd: Harnessing Our Digital Future*. New York: W. W. Norton & Company.

Mendis, D. (2021, August 24). When You Buy an NFT, You Don't Completely Own It – Here's Why. *The Conversation*, https://theconversation.com/when-you-buy-an-nft-you-dont-completely-own-it-heres-why-166445.

Moringiello, J. M. and Odinet, C. K. (2022). The Property Law of Tokens. *SSRN*, https://papers.ssrn.com/sol3/papers.cfm?abstract_id=3928901.

Morse, A. and Stein, S. (2022, January 21). The Metaverse is Just Getting Started: Here's What You Need to Know. *CNet*, https://www.cnet.com/tech/services-and-software/the-metaverse-is-everywhere-heres-what-you-need-to-know/.

Murphy, S. et al. (2021, July). The Metaverse: The Evolution of a Universal Digital Platform. *Norton Rose Fulbright*, https://www.nortonrosefulbright.com/en-us/knowledge/publications/5cd471a1/the-metaverse-the-evolution-of-a-universal-digital-platform.

Ong, T. (2021, June 17). Clothes that Don't Exist are Worth Big Money in the Metaverse. *Bloomberg*, https://www.bloomberg.com/news/features/2021-06-16/non-fungible-tokens-and-the-metaverse-are-digital-fashion-s-next-frontiers.

Pallavicini, F., Pepe, A. and Minissi, M. E. (2019). Gaming in Virtual Reality: What Changes in Terms of Usability, Emotional Response and Sense of Presence Compared to Non-Immersive Video Games? *Simulation & Gaming*, 50(2), 136–159.

Papacharissi, Z. (2015). *Affective Publics: Sentiment, Technology, and Politics*. Oxford: Oxford University Press.

Parkin, S. (2022, January 9). The Trouble with Roblox, the Video Game Empire Built on Child Labour. *The Guardian*, https://www.theguardian.com/games/2022/jan/09/the-trouble-with-roblox-the-video-game-empire-built-on-child-labour.

Perez, S. (2021, July 6). Roblox Partners with Sony Music to Connect Artists with Money-Making Activities in the Metaverse. *TechCrunch*, https://techcrunch.com/2021/07/06/roblox-partners-with-sony-music-to-connect-artists-with-money-making-activities-in-the-metaverse/.

Poell, T., Nieborg, D. and Duffy, B. E. (2022). *Platforms and Cultural Production*. Cambridge: Polity.

Procter, L. (2021). I Am/We Are: Exploring the Online Self-Avatar Relationship. *Journal of Communication Inquiry*, 45(1), 45–64.

Pryor, G. (2021, June 8). Will the New World of the Metaverse Be Governed by the Old Rules? *Games Industry*, https://www.gamesindustry.biz/articles/2021-06-08-new-world-old-rules-the-rise-of-the-metaverse.

Radoff, J. (2021a, April 7). The Metaverse Value-Chain. *Medium*, https://medium.com/building-the-metaverse/the-metaverse-value-chain-afcf9e09e3a7.

Radoff, J. (2021b, April 11). The Permissionless Metaverse. *Medium*, https://medium.com/building-the-metaverse/the-permissionless-metaverse-658872a35da4.

Ravenscraft, E. (2022, April 5). NFTs Are a Privacy and Security Nightmare. *Wired*, https://www.wired.com/story/nfts-privacy-security-nightmare/.

Rizzo, J. (2022, April 3). The Future of NFTs Lies with the Courts. *Wired*, https://www.wired.com/story/nfts-cryptocurrency-law-copyright/.

Rosenberg, L. (2022, January 27). The Danger of AI Micro-Targeting in the Metaverse. *Venture Beat*, https://venturebeat.com/2022/01/27/the-danger-of-ai-micro-targeting-in-the-metaverse/.

Scholz, J. and Duffy, K. (2018). We Are at Home: How Augmented Reality Reshapes Mobile Marketing and Consumer-Brand Relationships. *Journal of Retailing and Consumer Services*, 44, 11–23.

Stackpole, T. (2022, July–August). Exploring the Metaverse. *Harvard Business Review*, https://hbr.org/2022/07/exploring-the-metaverse.

Taylor, C. R. (2022). Research on Advertising in the Metaverse: A Call to Action. *International Journal of Advertising*, 21(3), 383–384.

Terry, Q. and Keeny, S. (2022). *The Metaverse Handbook: Innovating for the Internet's Next Tectonic Shift*. Hoboken: Wiley.

Tremayne, T. and Gill, R. (2021, July 7). We Need to Kick Big Tech out of the Metaverse. *Wired*, https://www.wired.co.uk/article/metaverse-big-tech.

Vaidhyanathan, S. (2018). *Anti-Social Media: How Facebook Disconnects Us and Undermines Democracy*. Oxford: Oxford University Press.

Virgilio, D. (2022, February 9). What Comparisons between *Second Life* and the Metaverse Miss. *Slate*, https://slate.com/technology/2022/02/second-life-metaverse-facebook-comparisons.html.

Wakefield, J. (2021, March 10). Roblox: How the Children's Game became a $30bn Bet on the Metaverse. *BBC*, https://www.bbc.com/news/technology-56345586.

Wiederhold, B. K. (2022). Ready (or Not) Player One: Initial Musing s on the Metaverse. *Cyberpsychology, Behavior, and Social Networking*, 25(1), 1–2.

Winters, T. (2021). *The Metaverse: Prepare Now for the Next Big Thing!* Independently published.

4 Doing Things
From Work to Sex

The metaverse is, of course, worthless without content and activities for people to engage in. In fact, the ultimate goal is for metaverse platforms to be all-encompassing – a gateway to work and learning, socialisation, leisure etc. – which ultimately means that 'when these things become so large and all-consuming, it doesn't leave much room for anything else' so that, ultimately, there is not going to be free time – if free time is considered to be something outside platform-mediated consumption practices (Webster 2021). Indeed, ways to earn and spend money will be inextricably intertwined. That, in addition to the obvious monetary returns for the companies involved, also will have the effect of locking users into particular platforms as spending accumulates. Such user investment, in terms of both money and effort, is driven by the importance of the performative and spectacular dimensions in the living out of the self. Nevertheless, the clearly pronounced outward projection represented through the avatar is also commodifying and consumptive. Moreover, as we move towards virtual sociality, new problems and challenges pertaining to user behaviour towards both AI-powered and human avatars present themselves, painting a much more mixed picture of life in the metaverse than most enthusiasts would entertain.

4.1 The Economic Side of the Metaverse

The metaverse must be seen as a domain of wide-ranging economic opportunities for both the companies creating it and the companies and brands intending to expand their audience. It is thus unsurprising that even a cursory search through metaverse-related trademark applications unveils established brands from sports teams to retailers, apparel manufacturers, celebrities, festivals, film franchises, and others applying to extend their intellectual property to the new domain (Jones 2022). This is already indicative of the metaverse being seen as a new domain of competition as technology develops and the user base expands. Nevertheless, this still leaves an

DOI: 10.4324/9781003355861-4

open question as to the economic activity *inside* the metaverse: after all, the money to spend on virtual goods in the metaverse must be earned, while platforms need to be able to continuously cash in on their user base.

Construction of the metaverse itself – of the various experiences and games that will constitute it – will in itself be a prominent activity, at least among a subset of the user base. That responds to a clear demand as well: because the metaverse needs large amounts of content to attract and be relevant to users, including but not limited to 'experiences like virtual amusement parks, virtual movie theaters, virtual concerts, virtual casinos, virtual schools, virtual conferences, anything you can name' (Sun 2021), outsourcing the creation of it all to users is a quick and financially efficient way to fill a platform with whatever is needed (Radoff 2021a). This content creator mode of participation in the virtual economy would likely, at least for some, acquire aspects of not just a hobby but also work, particularly if users can monetise their creations, e.g. *Roblox*-style. In this sense, virtual worlds would likely serve as venues for new forms of user creativity that are, nevertheless, heavily reliant on the platform on which they are being performed, including its policies and affordances – just as creativity performed on current online platforms is (Zhou, Leenders and Cong 2018).

Another kind of work inside the metaverse could be service provision broadly conceived, including, for example, venue design and preparation of entertainment for virtual events, which could become counterparts to, and at least partly replace, similar offline services, leading to the growth of a new class of metaverse gig workers (J. P. Morgan n.d.; see also Stackpole 2022). Likewise, people would work as creators of specific items to be sold to their fellow users, such as virtual items, skins, or entire buildings for owners of virtual real estate or companies creating their own experiences (Purdy 2022). Nevertheless, here the issue of future automation looms large. In a two-dimensional form, automated generation of content necessitating as little as a prompt is already making strides, with Open AI's *DALL-E* being (at the time of writing) the most recent headline-grabbing addition (Heaven 2022a). Such capacities will sooner or later move into three-dimensional space as well, making the position of human content creators increasingly precarious.

Still, even automation does not, as yet, eliminate human work – it just relegates and denigrates it as so-called 'ghost work', such as data labelling – the hidden, underpaid, and disempowered work enabling seemingly autonomous technologies (Hao and Hernández 2022) – that is, at least, until synthetic data (data generated by AI for AI's own use based on previous data) becomes the order of the day, making humans fully redundant (see e.g. Dankar and Ibrahim 2021; Lucini 2021; Heaven 2022b; Noble 2022). Meanwhile, a significantly more pressing threat is platform dependence and lack of monetisation transparency (and of the opportunity to bargain or otherwise affect it) for content creators – not to even mention the absence of social benefits and other perks typically associated with work (de Stefano, Aloisi and Contouris 2022). In other words, precariousness is likely to be the default condition of metaverse work – just as it already is across many parts of the digital economy.

Moreover, the matter of ownership looms large here: who is to own, or have rights to, user-generated content, and what remuneration would be offered to the user-creators. Thus far, ownership tends to be internal to proto-metaverse platforms and often lacks a financial aspect (i.e. is limited to prestige, ranking etc.), albeit some offer remuneration in an in-platform currency (e.g. based on the number of visits to such user-generated experiences) in order not just to entice users but also to stimulate internal economies. For platforms, there is a delicate balance: on the one hand, giving users more control and ownership tends to increase their willingness to create new content (Zhou, Leenders and Cong 2018: 58), but, on the other hand, the platform business model has always been based on retaining as much control and extracting as much value as possible (see e.g. Srnicek 2017; Couldry and Mejias 2019). Unsurprisingly, then, sceptics tend to observe that '[a]s things stand, this new reality is already shaping up along the familiar, proprietary, monopolistic lines' with metaverse platforms becoming increasingly more centralised, walled from outside, and more of an extension of the corporate interest of the big technology companies (Tremayne and Gill 2021). Hence, as already argued in this book, reliance on tried and tested models is more likely to prevail, even if they are somewhat repackaged to suit the new environment.

Considering employment practices more broadly, the metaverse would likely offer new work opportunities or significantly transform existing ones. Notably, the metaverse could make the remote office a mainstay. As Scott (2021) stresses, 'the metaverse suggests a new age for truly hybrid interactions', whereby 'we can transform the way we work and socialize on a fundamental scale', promising 'a new future for productivity and collaboration' (see also Radoff 2021a). Likewise, for Fowler (2021), 'one thing that's for certain is that people have discovered that working remotely opens the door to new opportunities for collaboration, growth and success' by allegedly making processes and practices more convenient, streamlined, and effective (see also Hackl and Buzzell 2022: 129–130). According to metaverse optimists, in a matter of years, 'attending meetings or job training in a physical space may seem an outdated practice – a folksy tale to be passed on to the grandchildren' (Sung-mi and Eun-seo 2021). Nevertheless, even amid this hype and optimism of truly global collaboration and remote work from any internet-connected beach anywhere in the world (see e.g. Sung-mi and

Eun-Seo 2021), some caution might be necessary. In fact, such future work might be much duller than it sounds, with the metaverse potentially enabling a ubiquity of work, with the virtual workplace available anywhere, at any time. That clearly is part of what e.g. Facebook/Meta implies with its idea of an 'infinite office': while infinite customisation and infinite geographical reach are part of what is on offer, infinite work is likely to be an outcome as well (Rubin 2021). The employees of such virtual offices will likely have to fight hard for their right not to visit the office part of the metaverse outside their working hours, just like checking one's corporate email outside working hours has only recently become less normal.

Virtual workplaces in the metaverse would likely be augmented through interactions between humans and AI-enabled 'colleagues', particularly performing assistant and advisory roles that are seen as 'low added value' (Purdy 2022), thereby discarding (both rhetorically and practically) much of human work, including that performed by early-career staff, and, as a result, raising issues with regard to access to employment. Simultaneously, metaverse offices would enable greater surveillance and downward pressure on wages and standards through increased outsourcing opportunities (de Stefano, Aloisi and Contouris 2022). In this sense, while it is possible that the metaverse would increase opportunities for workers in low-income countries to access jobs in high-income countries (Hackl and Buzzell 2021: 131; Hackl, Lueth and Di Bartolo 2022: 206; J. P. Morgan n.d.) or for others to enjoy greater freedom and flexibility (as per Schwab's (2017: 48) (in) famous defence of the gig economy), as also argued elsewhere in this book, it is more than likely to lead to new forms of exploitation, such as low-paid workers performing various 'microtasks' instead of accessing meaningful job opportunities. If meaningful job convergence *is* to take place, there are no guarantees that wages and work conditions would be those of high-income countries – instead, it is more likely for employment to become a race to the lowest common denominator, with workers under constant pressure to avoid being replaced with someone even cheaper (or having their role automated) and willing to accept longer working hours and less social security protection, if any.

Moving further, money is, of course, not only to be earned but also spent in the metaverse, with shopping, and consumption practices more broadly, serving as a prime example. This certainly does not come out of nowhere: especially since the pandemic, if not before, online shopping has already been normalised, with the metaverse merely accelerating the trend and enriching the experience, particularly in domains such as clothing and fashion, where the use of AR and VR for trying on, virtual brand experiences to entice customers, etc. are already proven concepts and are set to become commonplace (see e.g. Fowler 2021). The metaverse, then, offers an extension of customer enticement opportunities through, among other things, virtual malls and brand experiences (Winters 2021: 87). Nevertheless, while online shopping will certainly be the default option for purchasing in the metaverse (including purchasing virtual items and having their physical counterparts delivered to one's door), it is the truly metaversal items, such as virtual fashion, virtual real estate, and other kinds of virtual property, that will prove to be the truly disruptive factor (Hackl 2020; Snider 2021). Of course, brands sell in places where target consumers converge and sell the types of items that gain traction – hence, the metaverse and virtual items are a natural fit (Terry and Keeney 2022: 36–37).

Simultaneously, though, it is crucial to keep in mind that, when a purchase of a virtual item is made, the user is, in fact, simply acquiring 'a licence from the developers to use the items subject to the respective Terms of Service' (Zhou, Leenders and Cong 2018: 57). And while some authors (see, notably, Ball 2022: 59) would claim that, unless full ownership is given to users, the latter would be less willing to invest in virtual assets, such claims largely ignore the fact that individuals already invest heavily in digital and hybrid assets that they often do not fully own (for the technological permutations of ownership, see e.g. Noto La Diega 2022). Also, it is this caveat that could likely prevent seamless integration of different platforms into a single metaverse: while a user can bring their physical belongings from one (physical) place to another, the lack of full ownership would likely lock them (and their purchases) within a single metaverse platform. Therefore, the more the user has spent on virtual property and avatar customisations on one platform, the greater the disincentive to move elsewhere.

There is also a distinctly aesthetic element driving digital fashion and other goods – virtual designs can be completely unhinged, simply impossible to pull off the real world; hence, expression (of both designers and customers) becomes in principle unlimited (Palumbo 2021). It is also much easier to transform one's avatar than one's physical appearance (Oi 2021). Meanwhile, from a corporate perspective, there is a profit motive here as well: the cost per item is significantly lower without the need to produce the physical object, meaning higher profit margins even if purely digital items are sold at a discount (Palumbo 2021; see also Winters 2021: 86). As Hackl, Lueth and Di Bartolo (2022: 80) openly observe, 'digital assets can be cheap to produce and have immediate earning power'. Such absence of manufacturing can also be packaged in terms of sustainability, alleging that there is no resource usage or pollution or carbon footprint from shipping (Palumbo 2021; see also Winters 2021: 86). Nevertheless, the reality is much less clean since the design, rendering, storage (as part of avatar data), and movement calculation (of both the avatar and the garment) require significant energy resources (that are still typically generated from polluting non-renewable sources) and hardware, with the latter bringing resource exploitation and electronic waste into the mix. Also, while it is partly correct that savings are made on shipping costs (see e.g. Winters 2021: 86), the same cannot be said of so-called 'gas fees', i.e. processing charges pertaining to the Ethereum blockchain on which NFTs tend to operate (which can be excessive) (see e.g. Nover 2022). And, as for the alleged ethical advantages of virtual-only goods, while there may not be metaverse sweatshops in the conventional sense, concerns over exploitative digital work practices are already being raised (see e.g. Cipolla 2021; Spencer 2021; de Stefano, Aloisi and Contouris 2022; Parkin 2022).

Unsurprisingly, brands are discovering the benefits of positioning themselves in the metaverse and doing so early. The advice given to companies here is straightforward: '[i]f you make and sell products in the real world, there's probably a way to make and sell those products in virtual environments'; moreover, with the increase in immersiveness, the value attributed to such products is only expected to increase as well (Threekit n.d.). Of course, some of that metaverse promotionalism is overly simplistic: for example, simply asserting the vast and growing nature of the user base of current proto-metaverses without taking into account that businesses may have different target demographics that are unevenly represented within the user base (see e.g. Threekit n.d.) is simply naïve. Nevertheless, it is still clear that the new possibilities will have to be leveraged as much as possible, particularly as the metaverse increases opportunities for monetisation of an ever-larger array of daily activities. For example, in social interactions, there would be hybrid virtual–physical monetisation opportunities, such as jointly ordering food or drinks and having them delivered while virtually together inside the metaverse, despite being geographically far removed from each other (Wilser 2022).

All of the above constitutes good news for metaverse platforms as well: as the metaverse is used for purchase and consumption of goods, services, and experiences, there is a trove of data to be harvested while, if it is used for work, then the user base is likely to be upwardly affected as workers of metaverse offices would linger on for post-work socialisation and, then, continue to move to experiences, games, and other platform content, spending at least part of the revenue earned in the metaverse office. Indeed, it is part of the foreseeable business model to ensure that as much as possible of the income earned by the users (either using the metaverse as a medium for work – as an office – or working as content creators, or using it for immersive-experiential purposes only) is going to be spent in the platform. This trend is already clearly visible in many contemporary games that operate as assets continuously making money for their creators (as opposed to earlier, commodity-type games that would bring revenue through a one-time sale); now, users are already familiar with, and used to, what effectively is game-as-a-service, whereby relatively small – but frequent – payments must be made for various add-ons, seasonal passes, shortcuts, etc. (Bernevega and Gekker 2022: 51–52). In this way, long-term thinking prevails, whereby '*customer lifetime value*, or the total revenue generated by a user via in-game purchases, becomes central to the games' economic successes', as opposed to traditional sales figures (Bernevega and Gekker 2022: 52). In this way, games (or certain metaverse platform experiences or improvements, such as advertising-free services, priority passes, etc.) become either barely noticeable, as micro-transactions, or just one more subscription among many others (see, generally, Bernevega and Gekker 2022: 56). This can be seen as the new status quo of the platform model: so-called 'rentier capitalism' that 'uses mediation and enclosure to achieve extraction and control over its subjects' whereby continuous monetisation is achieved as 'an asset owner charges others to access that asset, just as a landlord charges tenants to rent a home the landlord owns' (Sadowski 2019). It is precisely the process of rendering 'X-as-a-service' that substitutes previous ways of creating corporate walled gardens through forced incompatibility with an analogous result via a subscription fee (Sadowski 2019; for an endorsement of a similar strategy for a metaverse, see e.g. Hackl, Lueth and Di Bartolo 2022: 116–117). Hence, users end up paying rent twice: in data and in actual currency (virtual or fiat), both reinforcing each other: data helps tailor services to make subscription more enticing, and subscription restricts cross-platform movement.

In the absence of subscription (or in the case of free-to-use versions of otherwise subscription-based products), extensive datafication (already evident in existing metaverse-related patents and applications), particularly of biometric data, and the sale of such data, combined with the placement of sponsored products and other forms of advertising, would undergird nominally 'free' service offerings (Murphy 2022). Indeed, the advertising-based business model of the current platforms is more than likely to be sustained in one form or another (J. P. Morgan n.d.), particularly through more sophisticated forms of in-metaverse user targeting, such as sponsored appearances of objects within metaverse experiences (Murphy 2022). Just as today, the success of a platform would, therefore, lie in getting right the balance between delighting users enough to come and stay but simultaneously annoying them enough to nudge them into the paid version.

Nevertheless, there is a further factor to note: in order for all such commercial opportunities to materialise, users need to perceive the metaverse as useful. While some will be shovelled in by work commitments, others will seek work here themselves, and others still will be motivated by socialisation or purely hedonic motives (such as immersive gaming experiences), that would still potentially leave a significant stratum of the population unaccounted for. Hence, the metaverse would need to span a host of uses in order to lure people in before locking users within proprietary walled gardens in one way or another. The idea here is that, just like with the office scenario above, users would join, or at least give a try, for one reason, and then their use would branch out across the entire spectrum of what metaverse platforms would end up offering. Moreover, such further uses would likely also offer additional, if minor, revenue streams through partnerships with institutions ranging from schools and universities to news media to museums and concert venues (or, particularly in the case of education and culture, with states' relevant government departments).

Indeed, education is another area that is likely to rank among the most significant applications of the metaverse. While much ink has been spilled over the benefits and shortcomings of online education during the pandemic, as Lee (2021) observes, particularly in higher education, the winners will be those institutions that prove to be the savviest investors in new technologies, thus attracting top talent regardless of where they are. Embracing the metaverse can enable such institutions to simulate in-person experiences and even overcome some of the biggest challenges in online learning, such as enabling 'scientific experiments, engineering prototyping and other hands-on activities' through virtual sessions (Lee 2021). Hence, it is asserted, '[t]he time has come to rebuild the curriculum and infrastructure for the world of the metaverse' (Lee 2021). After all, if future students are increasingly going to live their lives within the metaverse (and they are already growing up in proto-metaverse platforms; for example, the members of the main user base of *Roblox* are in their teens and younger), then traditional in-class educational experience will increasingly become counterintuitive. Also, moving into the metaverse would improve the experience of online study programs and expand the range of programs that are feasible online to include those necessitating an experiential and (with the appropriate development of haptics) hands-on element. That could help further globalise the education market, although perhaps with severe negative results to higher education institutions in less affluent countries and those enjoying lower academic reputation and clout, as such universities would either be unable to afford the development of metaverse curricula (and the connectivity to pull it off) or would struggle to attract students in a truly global market. The latter would also apply to less prestigious institutions in core educational markets.

Access to information will also be affected, getting a metaverse facelift and becoming a pull factor for users. To begin with, such a novel way of news consumption will necessitate a rethinking of journalistic practices.

Existing research on VR journalism has already highlighted a key concern around the emotion-evoking capacity of such content, which might open doors for manipulation (Uskali and Ikonen 2021) – even if the journalists themselves would not intentionally try to deceive the audiences. The additional emotional load due to perceived presence would impact the audience's cognitive processes in a way that is different from traditional journalistic reporting. A further issue with immersive content is the disappearance of authorship: whereas in traditional content it is easier for the audience to remain conscious of the constructed nature of what they encounter, immersiveness is likely to lead to over-ascribed authenticity and a greater sense of involvement (Johnson 2021). This can be described as a paradigm shift from story*telling* to story*living*, whereby, instead of telling a story, a journalist or other content creator almost magically creates a world to be lived in by the audience (Jones 2021). Moreover, although traditional storytelling tools, such as carefully selected shots and editing, become obsolete when the viewer can move within the location and choose their own point of view (Dooley 2021: 28, 32–33), there would still likely be curation in terms of choices of subjects, characters, and settings. Such highly immersive and experiential content would likely find itself an apt audience amid growing political polarisation and the rise in prominence of podcasts as a source of information and political opinion (Bratcher 2022; Dowling, Johnson and Ekdale 2022; Funk and Speakman 2022).

Another sector that is prone to reinvention in the metaverse is that of museums and galleries. While virtual exhibitions and tours are no longer a rarity, these have typically been considered as secondary offerings: a far less-than-perfect substitute for the 'real' experience of the physical artwork in a museum (Shirodkar 2021; see also Bolter, Engberg and MacIntyre 2021: 110). Nevertheless, virtual museum premises do hold numerous advantages over brick-and-mortar ones. These include accessibility (in terms of geographical and physical access), architectural fluidity (can be easily adjusted to any size or type of exhibition, unlike brick-and-mortar buildings), and the possibility of showing artworks from anywhere in the world simultaneously, including those that cannot be moved, such as murals or frescoes; likewise, such museums, owing to their virtual nature, can showcase artworks that have been irrevocably lost (Shirodkar 2021). Such museums can also feature artworks that are themselves digital-only, making the metaverse a key driver for digital art (Bolter, Engberg and MacIntyre 2021: 96; see also Winters 2021: 87). Simultaneously, such growth of virtual content would act as a pull factor, increasing the attractiveness of the metaverse to a new audience.

In addition to the above, it is also noteworthy that traditional forms of entertainment, such as music, could take on new forms. Here, some of the newly possible experiences will not simply be replacements of live performances – they will, in fact, be better, with augmented and physically unconstrained features; the same would potentially apply to theatre as well (Radoff 2021a). Such performances will also involve virtual musicians and other entertainers – and not just virtual representations of stars from the physical world (Oi 2021; Terry and Keeney 2022: 77–78). There is now an opportunity to create AI-powered virtual artists with unique styles and looks that do not even have to be or look anything like humans (Szalai 2021). Likewise, this constitutes multiple opportunities for creators of video games and animated films, book publishers, and other holders of stocks of imaginary characters to bring them to life in the metaverse through interactive experiences and dedicated AI-powered avatars (Terry and Keeney 2022: 78). As long as such virtual entertainers are fuelled by their audiences and maintained by their creators, they can be considered hardly less 'real' than their human-avatar counterparts.

It must, of course, be kept in mind that not all platforms are able to emulate *Fortnite*'s concert success and attract comparably large audiences (Tran 2022). Still, the allure of becoming the gateway to entertainment would likely be sufficient for most metaverse platforms to throw their hats in. Likewise, partnerships could be forged with media and entertainment companies (such as film and music studios) for joint hybrid or purely virtual content offerings – especially if potentially thorny matters, such as the use of intellectual property, are solved (see e.g. Morgan 2021; Hughes 2021; Ball 2022; Moore 2022; Osborne Clarke 2022; Ramos 2022; Sun-hwa 2022; Wilson 2022). Entertainment and leisure should, however, be understood in a broad sense to include, for example, a further blending of sports and what is now known as esports, blurring the line between virtual and physical performance, spectatorship, and participation (see e.g. Hackl and Buzzell 2021: 192; Brand et al. 2022; Quinn 2022; Tsui 2022). Moreover, thinking about leisure and experiences should not be limited to mere virtualisations and enhancements of already existing online (or video gaming) practices – instead, immersively acting out fantasies and never-done-before endeavours would very likely prove popular as well (Hackl, Lueth and Di Bartolo 2022: 116).

Notably, the metaverse could also serve as a substitution for travel (Radoff 2021a), particularly if (or once) tourist venues and attractions acquire a metaverse presence. Especially in times of heightened attention being paid to the carbon footprint generated by the travel industry, the metaverse could be seen as a more attractive (and ethical) option – particularly if the metaverse's own environmental concerns are glossed over. Nevertheless, a controversy can be foreseen here owing to the importance of the tourism industry to the economies of many countries. Hence, when transferring sights and attractions into a virtual form, the revenue-generating effects of tourism that trickle down across multiple sectors would be lost or require a metaverse rethink, which might not always be feasible, particularly in poorer countries. A far less controversial travel substitute would be conferences and events, creating the sense of in-person participation without physical co-presence (Bolter, Engberg and MacIntyre 2021: 119; Winters 2021: 87–88, 96–97). Nevertheless, regardless of the options that become dominant, the overall takeaway is that there would be plentiful potential uses of the metaverse to both directly engage users in economic practices and to lure them in beforehand.

4.2 Acting and Feeling in the Metaverse

The goal of the metaverse is to ultimately become an experience in every sense of the term, including in terms of physical sensing. For almost any type of metaverse use, the ability to touch and feel – haptic technology – is crucial. Hence, development of haptic materials and devices that would be sufficiently comfortable to be worn and sensitive enough to convey physical sensation is one of the main research priorities when it comes to the metaverse (Goode 2021a; Shead 2021). Notably, the spectrum of technological solutions already under development is itself rather broad and encompasses not just wearable haptic technology but also tools and devices that use e.g. ultrasonic waves to simulate touch, thereby enabling tactile experiences (Takahashi 2022). Clearly, though, the computing power necessary to detect, translate, and convey physical sensation will only further add to the energy consumption – and, therefore, environmental footprint – of the metaverse.

What is absolutely clear, though, is that the metaverse would end up functioning as a constellation of new and updated technologies of the self in a part-Foucauldian sense (for the latter, see e.g. Nilson 1998; Kelly 2013). Still, it must be kept in mind that the range of possibilities is structured by platform affordances and thus also partly subjected to matters of power and control. Of course, already on traditional social media, self-representation on a profile could have been understood as 'an explicit act of writing yourself into being in a digital environment' (boyd 2011: 43). Similarly, for Broadbent and Lobet-Maris (2015: 118), interactions within a digital environment are 'marked by the constant necessity to become visible' or a 'quest for visibility' – a constant effort and striving to get attention, 'to occupy the mental space of others and to stay on top of the competition'. In short, the situation is very similar for both individuals and brands. In an important way, then, the digital is a domain of universalised strategic self-crafting (Goodwin et al. 2016: 10).

Effectively, such relentless self-representational drive has become the norm in what Ibrahim (2019: 1116) calls a 'performative society' that arises at the conjunction of 'the spectacle with the commodification of the self' as 'the narcissistic interweaves with the spectacular'. The performative element, therefore, takes precedence on digital platforms (Ibrahim 2019: 1116). While it is true that people have often relied on self-performance prior to the emergence of digital interactions as well, digital media, being representative by definition (we do not encounter one another directly but only through how we display ourselves in and through the medium), elevates it to a whole new level (Szulc 2019: 260). This necessitates intentional and strategic profile curation and, indeed, constant work on the self by permanently polishing one's online image (see e.g. Courtenay-Smith 2018). The latter is even more acute when we move from intervention-based self-representation that takes place through separate and strategic acts of uploading information, images, or videos to persistent performance as a virtually present avatar that is constantly projecting (a version of) the self that may, or may not, resemble the person behind it.

Another factor of note is the ascription of value: as, in the digital environment particularly, there is little else available in terms of approximating the relative standing of individuals apart from constant comparisons of the effectiveness (and spectacularity) of their self-representations, the consequence, almost unavoidably, is profile inflation (Zuboff 2019: 462) or, in the metaverse, avatar inflation – a self-perpetuating process whereby investments in avatars – in terms of appearance, virtual dwellings, reputational value, etc. – trigger investments by others which, in turn, trigger investment by those who had done so previously but are now lagging behind, and so on. In a somewhat similar fashion, Ibrahim (2018: 37) discusses 'the emergence of a profile economy', whereby the value of a person is ascribed through the gaze of others laid on their digital profiles – or avatars. Simultaneously, then, this means the erasure of the boundary between the private and the public 'as we offer ourselves as commodities for the consumption of others (Ibrahim 2018: 2). In fact, this commodifying, consumptive nature of the self is paramount in the sense that it is one of the core value generators for online platforms – an important reason why people visit and return is the opportunity to consume others, and not just in a passive, voyeuristic sense but interactively so.

The self, then, becomes entrepreneurial in the sense that it necessitates continuous labour and promotion in a highly competitive environment (Arriagada and Ibáñez 2020: 2–3) whereby the avatar becomes a crucial enabler of self-expression and impression (Hackl and Buzzell 2021: 69). What is peculiar, though, is the merger of roles as one is simultaneously an entrepreneur and the product made by that entrepreneur, the aim being to produce a self that manifests as high a consumption value as possible. However, just like in many other entrepreneurial environments, humans face a growing competition from AI. In this case, human avatars would have to compete for attention with AI-enabled virtual personalities and influencers that, being based on audience data, would likely have an upper hand in attracting the value-ascribing gaze (Sands et al. 2022). After all, there is growing evidence that humans are fully capable of establishing parasocial (or as-if-social) relations with wholly distant others – be they media personalities or, for that matter, virtual influencers (see e.g. Block and Lovegrove 2021: 271–272; Miao et al. 2022; Mrad, Ramadan and Nasr 2022). In the end, with the growing capacities of robots, 'robotic' may no longer be a denigration or an insult (Winterson 2021: 180). Instead, (virtual) robots may offer just another socialisation opportunity – and one that may, under some circumstances, even seem preferable.

Indeed, socialisation is best seen as a deeply engrained evolutionary human need that has long served as a tool to ensure survival through dependence and belonging; there is even a broad emotional spectrum to support and undergird it: 'the joy of acceptance and agony of rejection' (Storr 2021: 1). The two corresponding drives – the desire to bring about acceptance and that to avoid rejection – would also play a significant role in driving metaverse behaviour and spending. After all, status (maximisation of acceptance and minimisation of rejection) is the force that drives 'every social interaction, every contribution we make to work, love or family life and every internet post' as well as 'how we dress, how we speak and what we believe' (Storr 2021: 2). In this sense, one could also hardly speak of an independent self, unconnected to the wider social stratum – as Nowotny (2022: 76) stresses, 'we are what others see us to be', whereby 'our identities are shaped by the networks through which we are connected with others; and, increasingly for us, these networks are digital'. The latter, then, has two interlinked meanings: on the one hand, the digitality of networks pertains to the fact that communication and interaction are literally enabled by and take place through digital platforms and network infrastructure, thus tying the human and the digital together; on the other hand, there is also a deeper sense, particularly pertaining to the metaverse, whence sociality takes place through digital representations (avatars) and even not all of such avatars stand in for physical human persons.

The social and persistent nature of the metaverse means that communication and interaction based around jointly frequented environments will be one of the main uses and purposes of the metaverse (Benford 2021). Such environments, however, will involve problematic issues with regard to interactions, especially with AI-powered avatars. Looking ahead, such actors will likely be of varied sophistication: some will be hardly (if at all) distinguishable from real humans, while others would perform entertainment and service roles within in-platform experiences (Ong 2021), somewhat similar to non-player characters in today's games. This will open up new ethical domains – in terms of (in)appropriate behaviours towards synthetic avatars – as well as new avenues for influencing people, particularly through the use of AI-powered agents that leverage user data for manipulative purposes. This would likely include intensification of astroturfing behaviours – practices already widespread on today's social media, whereby fake (usually automated) accounts are being used to create a misleading impression of grassroots engagement and dominant opinion (see e.g. Chan 2022). As humans have a tendency to defer to what seems to be the dominant opinion and/or moral code, the manipulative use of such artificial personas can be seen to constitute a serious societal and political threat (Chan 2022). Indeed, manipulation through AI-driven agents specifically created for social engineering purposes would be one of the likely threats brought about by the metaverse; as such agents would be able to parse our data and adjust to emotional states in real time, they are likely to be efficient in their manipulative capacities (Rosenberg 2022; see also Block and Lovegrove 2021). Other issues to consider include romantic relationships with and emotional reliance on AI agents (Bardhan 2022) that either develop accidentally or as part of a deliberate plot to, for example, defraud the human user. There is, consequently, a need for transparency and disclosure as to the actual nature of AI-powered avatars.

Further complicating the ethics landscape is the question of how AI avatars are to be treated. Already existing, highly troubling examples include users (men) creating AI 'girlfriends' and not only abusing them but also publicly posting such interactions (Bardhan 2022). As such actions move from screen-mediated interactions into the metaverse and with the addition of haptic technologies, abuse is likely to become more than verbal. In addition, since these abusive interactions appear to closely follow the patterns typical of real-life domestic abuse, in addition to the more abstract problem of human–AI interaction, it can have inter-human implications as well, reinforcing misogynistic attitudes and becoming a practice ground for the abuse of real-life women (Bardhan 2022). More broadly, though, harassment seems to already constitute a problem in the proto-metaverse platforms of today, with (as argued in the chapters that follow) significant adverse effects for the human users. Nevertheless, solutions typically tend to be reactive rather than proactive (i.e. developed *after* publicised negative user experiences as opposed to being foreseen), likely pointing to the blind spots of a generally homogeneous (white male) developer community and underscoring that a secure metaverse is impossible 'without a diverse group of inventors, architects, and thought leaders [...] participating in its creation'

(Goode 2021b). This, however, is one aspect of metaverse democratisation that is conveniently glossed over in the largely celebratory accounts.

Continuing on the matter of interactions, it would be difficult to imagine pornography (and, with the development of appropriate haptics, sex) not becoming a prominent feature of the metaverse (Bolter, Engberg and MacIntyre 2021: 94–95). Once again, the key selling point here is immersion and richness of experience, whereby 'the viewer is *in* the scene' – the position is no longer voyeuristic but, instead, one of a participant (Rubin 2020: 203). With that in mind, sexualised – and even pornographic – experiences are guaranteed to move into various metaverse platforms as well. In fact, steps have already been made in this direction, as illustrated by Meta's shift in position to create an adult-only tag for user-generated content, allowing for sexually explicit experiences – a type of content it had previously banned (Clark 2022). This might also be a tacit acknowledgement of something even deeper – that adult content is nothing less than an important pull factor driving users towards the metaverse – not too dissimilar from the role it has played on the conventional internet (see e.g. Moynihan 2018; Khalili 2021). Quite likely, though, virtual pornography (and virtual sex) will move beyond human performers (and partners) – after all, it transpires that human and nonhuman characters are similarly effective in terms of activating emotional responses (Stiegler 2021: 92). Moreover, as virtual agents can be pre-programmed towards any preferences, desires, and peculiarities of taste, they would also be likely seen as more fulfilling than humans in terms of both the emotional side of the relationship and offering the ability to act out fantasies and desires that may be too niche for an absolute majority of potential human partners.

It transpires that arousal is possible even with minimal and very primitive haptic technology (Aleksandrovich and Gomes 2020), but, when combined with the rapid growth and advances in sextech, and particularly in the domain of teledildonics (remotely operated sex toys), virtual sex can be expected to become more than a quirk (McArthur and Twist 2019; Drouin 2022). Even though problems around technology, privacy, and the necessary connection speeds abound (see e.g. Hay 2021), normalisation of virtual intimate experiences should happen relatively soon. Indeed, with further technological developments, morally, ethically, and legally sensitive issues are going to arise: for example, whom one can have virtual sex with and what counts as consent (Susskind 2018: 13). Also, as the gender on the avatar may not necessarily be the same as the gender of the person behind it, choices will have to be made as to transparency with regard to the physical gender of the person one is having virtual sex with. The popularity of virtual sex would likely also build on the growing industry of AI sex dolls (Winterson 2021). In the metaverse, artificial partners would no longer even have to be physical but merely based on graphics and haptics. A further factor of note is, again, the potential for objectification and normalisation of abuse: the sex doll, physical or virtual, cannot say no, regardless of one's behaviour towards it. But there are also further issues pertaining to humans as well – for example, the addition of image- and avatar-morphing software introduces the ability to change appearance and identity, which might not even be bound to being human but those of anything from animals to fantasy creatures; and, if something reminiscent of virtual zoophilia is troubling, it is also likely that such activities would involve avatars of adults posing as minors (Volpicelli 2021).

In terms of other lifestyle options and choices, an important proposition of the metaverse is its capacity to make formerly scarce experiences and lifestyles abundant (Radoff 2021b; see also Hackl and Buzzell 2021: 169). Whether that is entrance to a coveted concert or sailing a private yacht across the Caribbean, virtually any activity and experience can be simulated, if not here and now, then with foreseeable developments in haptic technology in mind. While, under some interpretations, such freedom of choice could be liberating, in actual practice it would likely mean alienation from actual living conditions – a synthetic substitute that would only diminish the demand for real social change (Gault 2021). Hence, '[i]n a world of increasing wealth inequality, environmental disaster, and political instability, why not sell everyone a device that whisks them away to a virtual world free of pain and suffering?' (Gault 2021). Similarly, for Bogost (2021), the metaverse makes it possible to forego the daily irritants in favour of more sanitised and controllable virtual environments. Here, again, one encounters the idea of escape sold by technology billionaires: in this case, not the fantasy of physically leaving the Earth altogether, but the virtual reality of a fantasy world.

With the above uses in mind, it is not surprising that prices for virtual land are soaring (Frank 2022). Virtual plots of land can now be transformed into virtual shops, offices and conference facilities, museums and concert halls, casinos and nightclubs, fashion stores, etc. (*The Economist* 2022). Such uptake should not be surprising given that these are virtual venues for virtual humans (avatars) to spend real money (*The Economist* 2022). As virtual worlds abound, with multiple options for purchasing virtual real estate now being available, the big investors are, at least for now, hedging their bets across platforms (*The Economist* 2022). Nevertheless, as previously stressed in relation to the metaverse in general, concentration should be expected, as typically is the case with any domain that enters a platformisation stage. Once that happens, much of the current investment will have to be written off as the platforms in which it had been made get shovelled aside by those that come to dominate. Ultimately, the lucky ones cash in significantly by becoming the only players in town – a characteristic technology boom and bust cycle. In this sense, the enthusiasts' claims that 'you cannot lose', whichever platform one invests in (see, notably, Terry and Keeney 2022: 134), do not stand up to scrutiny.

In the end, what we are witnessing here is the conflation of work and play; however, this conflation is out of balance – and it is not gamification of work as is often asserted. Instead, what we are witnessing is the 'workification' of everything, from the building of fantasy worlds and experiences to playing them to creation and performance of a persona (avatar) – in the end, 'instead of offering digital liberation and ownership, the metaverse is offering more responsibilities without a promotion' (Stackpole 2022). Ultimately, work, both in an economic and self-centric sense, would become ever-present reality.

Bibliography

Aleksandrovich, A. and Gomes, L. M. (2020). Shared Multisensory Sexual Arousal in Virtual Reality (VR) Environments. *Paladyn, Journal of Behavioral Robotics*, 11(1), 279–289.

Arriagada, A. and Ibáñez, F. (2020). You Need at Least On Picture Daily, if not, You're Dead: Content Creators and Platform Evolution in the Social Media Ecology. *Social Media + Society*, doi: 10.1177/2056305120944624.

Bardhan, A. (2022, January 18). Men Are Creating Virtual Girlfriends and then Verbally Abusing Them. *Futurism*, https://futurism.com/chatbot-abuse.

Ball, M. (2022). *The Metaverse and How It Will Revolutionize Everything*. New York: Liveright Publishing.

Benford, S. (2021, November 4). Metaverse: Five Things to Know – And What It Could Mean for You. *The Conversation*, https://theconversation.com/metaverse-five-things-to-know-and-what-it-could-mean-for-you-171061.

Bernevega, A. and Gekker, A. (2022). The Industry of Landlords: Exploring the Assetization of the Triple-A Game. *Games and Culture*, 17(1), 47–69.

Block, E. and Lovegrove, R. (2021). Discordant Storytelling, 'Honest Fakery', Identity Peddling: How Uncanny CGI Characters are Jamming Public Relations and Influencer Practices. *Public Relations Inquiry*, 10(3), 265–293.

Bogost, I. (2021, October 21). The Metaverse is Bad. *The Atlantic*, https://www.theatlantic.com/technology/archive/2021/10/facebook-metaverse-name-change/620449/.

Bolter, J. D., Engberg, M. and MacIntyre, B. (2021). *Reality Media: Augmented and Virtual Reality*. Cambridge and London: The MIT Press.

boyd, D. (2011). Social Network Sites as Networked Publics: Affordances, Dynamics, and Implications. In Z. Papacharissi (ed.) *A Networked Self: Identity, Community, and Culture on Social Network Sites* (pp. 39–58). London: Routledge.

Brand, R. L. et al. (2022, June 23). Sports in the Metaverse: Key Considerations. *Arent Fox Schiff*, https://www.afslaw.com/perspectives/alerts/sports-the-metaverse-key-considerations.

Bratcher, T. R. (2022). Toward a Deeper Discussion: A Survey Analysis of Podcasts and Personalized Politics. *Atlantic Journal of Communication*, 30(2), 188–199.

Broadbent, S. and Lobet-Maris, C. (2015). Towards a Grey Ecology. In L. Floridi (ed.) *The Onlife Manifesto: Being Human in a Hyperconnected Era* (pp. 111–124). Cham: Springer.

Chan, J. (2022). Online Astroturfing: A Problem Beyond Disinformation. *Philosophy and Social Criticism*, doi: 10.1177/01914537221108467.

Cipolla, A. (2021, November 29). Work in the Metaverse: A Future Problem? *Latin American Post*, https://latinamericanpost.com/39140-work-in-the-metaverse-a-future-problem.

Clark, M. (2022, July 22). Meta Adds an 18 and up Tag in Horizon Worlds, Opening the Door to Mature VR Content. *The Verge*, https://www.theverge.com/2022/7/22/23274676/meta-horizon-worlds-mature-content-18-plus-tag?fbclid=IwAR1XTP1psYlJAjbqoibgqYc8bH7BTdckJdHdgeyaE7BQabemU-zNz4V7Oog.

Couldry, N. and Mejias, U. A. (2019). *The Costs of Connection: How Data Is Colonizing Human Life and Appropriating It for Capitalism*. Stanford: Stanford University Press.

Courtenay-Smith, N. (2018). *Stand Out Online*. London: Piatkus.

Dankar, F. and Ibrahim, M. (2021). Fake It till You Make It: Guidelines for Effective Synthetic Data Generation. *Applied Sciences*, 11(5), 1–18.

de Stefano, V., Aloisi, A. and Contouris, N. (2022, February 1). The Metaverse Is a Labour Issue. *Social Europe*, https://socialeurope.eu/the-metaverse-is-a-labour-issue.

Dooley, K. (2021). *Cinematic Virtual Reality: A Critical Study of 21st Century Approaches and Practices*. London: Palgrave Macmillan.

Dowling, D. O., Johnson, P. R., Ekdale, B. (2022). Hijacking Journalism: Legitimacy and Metajournalistic Discourse in Right-Wing Podcasts. *Media and Communication*, 10(3), 1–11.

Drouin, M. (2022, February 21). Immersive VR is the Next Frontier of Sexual Experiences. *Medium*, https://onezero.medium.com/immersive-vr-is-the-next-frontier-of-sexual-experiences-d0e43074dce9.

Fowler, G. (2021, November 15). The Future of Work and Society in the Metaverse. *Forbes*, https://www.forbes.com/sites/forbesbusinessdevelopmentcouncil/2021/11/15/the-future-of-work-and-society-in-the-metaverse/?sh=15e3f68f77e4.

Frank, A. (2022, February 1). Metaverse Real Estate Sales Top $500 Million, and Are Projected to Double this Year. *CNBC*, https://www.cnbc.com/2022/02/01/metaverse-real-estate-sales-top-500-million-metametric-solutions-says.html.

Funk, M. and Speakman, B. (2022). Centrist Language, Camouflaged Ideology: Assembled Text-Based Content on Mainstream and Ideological News Podcasts. *Journalism Studies*, doi: 10.1080/1461670X.2022.2094820.

Gault, M. (2021, February 15). Billionaires See VR as a Way to Avoid Radical Social Change. *Wired*, https://www.wired.com/story/billionaires-use-vr-avoid-social-change/.

Goode, L. (2021a, November 16). Facebook Reaches for More Realistic VR with Haptic Gloves. *Wired*, https://www.wired.com/story/facebook-haptic-gloves-vr/.

Goode, L. (2021b, August 27). The Architects of the Metaverse Need to Read the Virtual Room. *Wired*, https://www.wired.com/story/plaintext-architects-metaverse-diversity/.

Goodwin, I. et al. (2016). Precarious Popularity: Facebook Drinking Photos, the Attention Economy, and the Regime of the Branded Self. *Social Media + Society*, doi:10.1177/2056305116628889.

Greengard, S. (2019). *Virtual Reality*. Cambridge: The MIT Press.

Hackl, C. (2020, July 5). The Metaverse is Coming and It's a Very Big Deal. *Forbes*, https://www.forbes.com/sites/cathyhackl/2020/07/05/the-metaverse-is-coming--its-a-very-big-deal/?sh=4df2bc2b440f.

Hackl, C. and Buzzell, J. (2021). *The Augmented Workforce* (2nd ed.). North Kansas City: Renown Publishing.

Hackl, C., Lueth, D. and Di Bartolo, T. (2022). *Navigating the Metaverse: A Guide to Limitless Possibilities in a Web 3.0 World*. Hoboken: Wiley.

Hao, K. and Hernández, A. P. (2022, April 20). How the AI Industry Profits from Catastrophe. *MIT Technology Review*, https://www.technologyreview.com/2022/04/20/1050392/ai-industry-appen-scale-data-labels/.

Hay, M. (2021, January 11). How to Watch VR Porn: Everything You Need to Know. *Mashable*, https://mashable.com/article/virtual-reality-vr-porn-how-to-watch.

Heaven, W. D. (2022a, April 6). This Horse-Riding Astronaut Is a Milestone in AI's Journey to Make Sense of the World. *MIT Technology Review*, https://www.technologyreview.com/2022/04/06/1049061/dalle-openai-gpt3-ai-agi-multimodal-image-generation/.

Heaven, W. D. (2022b, February 23). Synthetic Data for AI. *MIT Technology Review*, https://www.technologyreview.com/2022/02/23/1044965/ai-synthetic-data-2/.

Hughes, N. C. (2021, November 23). Is the Metaverse the Future of Entertainment? *Cyber News*, https://cybernews.com/editorial/is-the-metaverse-the-future-of-entertainment/.

Ibrahim, Y. (2018). *Production of the 'Self' in the Digital Age*. London: Palgrave Macmillan.

Ibrahim, Y. (2019). The Vernacular of Photobombing: The Aesthetics of Transgression. *Convergence*, 25(5–6), 1111–1122.

J. P. Morgan. (n.d.). Opportunities in the Metaverse: How Businesses Can Explore the Metaverse and Navigate the Hype vs Reality, https://www.jpmorgan.com/content/dam/jpm/treasury-services/documents/opportunities-in-the-metaverse.pdf.

Johnson, D. G. (2021). Promises and Perils in Immersive Journalism. In T. Uskali, A. Gynnild, S. Jones and E. Sirkkunen (eds.) *Immersive Journalism as Storytelling: Ethics, Production, and Design* (pp. 71–81). London: Routledge.

Jones, O. (2022, February 8). The Rise in NFT and Metaverse-Related Trademark Applications. *JDSupra*, https://www.jdsupra.com/legalnews/the-rise-in-nft-and-metaverse-related-2940820/.

Jones, S. (2021). It's Not Just About Empathy: Going Beyond the Empathy Machine in Immersive Journalism. In T. Uskali et al. (eds.), *Immersive Journalism as Storytelling: Ethics, Production, and Design* (pp. 82–95). London: Routledge.

Kelly, M. G. E. (2013). Foucault, Subjectivity, and Technologies of the Self. In C. Falzon, T. O'Leary and J. Sawicki (eds.) *A Companion to Foucault* (pp. 510–525). Hoboken: Blackwell Publishing.

Khalili, J. (2021, July 13). These Are the Most Popular Websites Right Now – and they Might Just Surprise You. *Tech Radar*, https://www.techradar.com/news/porn-sites-attract-more-visitors-than-netflix-and-amazon-youll-never-guess-how-many.

Lee, K. H. (2021, May 10). The Educational 'Metaverse' is Coming. *Times Higher Education*, https://www.timeshighereducation.com/campus/educational-metaverse-coming.

Lucini, F. (2021, October 20). The Real Deal about Synthetic Data. *MIT Sloan Management Review*, https://sloanreview.mit.edu/article/the-real-deal-about-synthetic-data/.

McArthur, M. and Twist, M. (2019, February 11). Robots and Virtual Reality are the Future of Sex. *The Independent*, https://www.independent.co.uk/news/science/sex-love-robot-virtual-reality-digisexual-future-vr-relationships-a8773391.html.

Miao, F., Kozlenkova, I. V., Wang, H., Xie, T. and Palmatier, R. W. (2022). An Emerging Theory of Avatar Marketing. *Journal of Marketing*, 86(1), 67–90.

Moore, P. (2022, May 4). Is the Metaverse a Boon for the Entertainment Industry? *Atos*, https://atos.net/en/blog/is-the-metaverse-a-boon-for-the-entertainment-industry.

Morgan, C. M. (2021, September 1). Intellectual Property in the World of the Metaverse. *Reed Smith*, https://www.reedsmith.com/en/perspectives/2021/09/intellectual-property-in-the-world-of-the-metaverse.

Moynihan, Q. (2018, September 30). Internet Users Access Porn Websites More than Twitter, Wikipedia and Netflix. *Business Insider*, https://www.businessinsider.com/internet-users-access-porn-more-than-twitter-wikipedia-and-netflix-2018-9?r=US&IR=T.

Mrad, M., Ramadan, Z. and Nasr, L. I. (2022). Computer-Generated Influencers: The Rise of Digital Personalities. *Marketing Intelligence & Planning*, doi: 10.1108/MIP-12-2021-0423.

Murphy, H. (2022, January 18). Facebook Patents Reveal How It Intends to Cash in on the Metaverse. *Financial Times*, https://www.ft.com/content/76d40aac-034e-4e0b-95eb-c5d34146f647.

Nilson, H. (1998). *Michel Foucault and the Games of Truth*. London: Palgrave Macmillan.

Noble, A. (2022, May 9). What Is Synthetic Data, and how Can It Advance Research and Development? *The Royal Society*, https://royalsociety.org/blog/2022/05/synthetic-data/.

Noto La Diega, G. (2022). *Internet of Things and the Law: Legal Strategies for Consumer-Centric Smart Technologies*. London: Routledge.

Nover, S. (2022, May 3). Bored Ape Yacht Club's NFTs Cost Buyers $181 Million in 'Gas' Fees. *Quartz*, https://qz.com/2161193/bored-ape-yacht-clubs-nfts-cost-181-million-in-gas-fees/.

Nowotny, H. (2022). *In AI We Trust: Power, Illusion and Control of Predictive Algorithms*. Cambridge: Polity Press.

Oi, M. (2021, December 23). Is this the World's Largest Fashion Show? *BBC*, https://www.bbc.com/news/business-59558921.

Ong, A. (2021, October 27). This Company Is Making Digital Humans to Serve the Metaverse. *The Verge*, https://www.theverge.com/2021/10/27/22746679/soul-machines-metaverse-digital-humans-labor.

Osborne Clarke. (2022, April 28). IP and the Metaverse: Ownership and Infringement of Rights, https://www.osborneclarke.com/insights/ip-and-metaverse-ownership-and-infringement-rights.

Palumbo, J. (2021, December 21). Digital Dress Codes: What will We Wear in the Metaverse? *CNN*, https://edition.cnn.com/style/article/metaverse-digital-fashion/index.html.

Parkin, S. (2022, January 9). The Trouble with Roblox, the Video Game Empire Built on Child Labour. *The Guardian*, https://www.theguardian.com/games/2022/jan/09/the-trouble-with-roblox-the-video-game-empire-built-on-child-labour.

Purdy, M. (2022, April 5). How the Metaverse Could Change Work. *Harvard Business Review*, https://hbr.org/2022/04/how-the-metaverse-could-change-work.

Quinn, S. (2022, April 26). How the Metaverse Could Unlock Sustainable Revenue Models for Esports. *VentureBeat*, https://venturebeat.com/datadecisionmakers/how-the-metaverse-could-unlock-sustainable-revenue-models-for-esports/.

Radoff, J. (2021a, May 27). The Experiences of the Metaverse. *Medium*, https://medium.com/building-the-metaverse/the-experiences-of-the-metaverse-2126a7899020.

Radoff, J. (2021b, April 7). The Metaverse Value-Chain. *Medium*, https://medium.com/building-the-metaverse/the-metaverse-value-chain-afcf9e09e3a7.

Ramos, A. (2022, June). The Metaverse, NFTs and IP rights: To Regulate or not to Regulate? *WIPO Magazine*, https://www.wipo.int/wipo_magazine/en/2022/02/article_0002.html.

Rosenberg, L. (2022, January 27). The Danger of AI Micro-Targeting in the Metaverse. *Venture Beat*, https://venturebeat.com/2022/01/27/the-danger-of-ai-micro-targeting-in-the-metaverse/.

Rubin, P. (2020). *Future Presence: How Virtual Reality Is Changing Human Connection, Intimacy, and the Limits of Ordinary Life*. New York: Harper One.

Rubin, P. (2021, August 19). Horizon Workrooms: Facebook's Metaverse Is a VR Meetaverse. *Wired*, https://www.wired.com/story/facebook-horizon-workrooms-metaverse/.

Sadowski, J. (2019, April 4). Landlord 2.0: Tech's New Rentier Capitalism. *Medium*, https://onezero.medium.com/landlord-2-0-techs-new-rentier-capitalism-a0bfe491b463.

Sands, S. et al. (2022). Unreal Influence: Leveraging AI in Influencer Marketing. *European Journal of Marketing*, doi: 10.1108/EJM-12-2019-0949.

Schwab. K. (2017). *The Fourth Industrial Revolution*. London: Portfolio.

Scott, R. (2021, June 2). The Metaverse Workplace: Get Ready for Virtual Work. *XR Today*, https://www.xrtoday.com/mixed-reality/the-metaverse-workplace-get-ready-for-virtual-work/.

Shead, S. (2021, November 21). Mark Zuckerberg Says a New Skin-Like Material Could Support Metaverse Ambitions. *CNBC*, https://www.cnbc.com/2021/11/01/mark-zuckerberg-says-a-new-material-could-support-metaverse-ambitions.html.

Shirodkar, S. (2021, October 18). Virtual Museums Challenge the Art World's Status Quo. *Wired*, https://www.wired.com/story/pandemic-changes-art-experience/.

Snider, M. (2021, April 21). From Minecraft to Zoom Calls, We've All Spent Much of the Pandemic on Our Screens: But Are We Ready for the Metaverse? *USA Today*, https://eu.usatoday.com/in-depth/tech/2021/04/21/minecraft-roblox-fortnite-nft-creating-metaverse/7000381002/.

Spencer, M. (2021, December 22). Roblox Is Setting up the Metaverse for a Child Labor Gig Economy. *LinkedIn*, https://www.linkedin.com/pulse/roblox-setting-up-metaverse-child-labor-gig-economy-michael-spencer-/?trk=public_post-content_share-article.

Srnicek, N. (2017). *Platform Capitalism*. Cambridge: Polity Press.

Stackpole, T. (2022, July–August). Exploring the Metaverse. *Harvard Business Review*, https://hbr.org/2022/07/exploring-the-metaverse.

Stiegler, C. (2021). *The 360° Gaze: Immersions in Media, Society, and Culture*. Cambridge: The MIT Press.

Storr, W. (2021). *The Status Game: On Social Position and How We Use It*. London: William Collins.

Sun, C. (2021, November 24). Architecting in the Metaverse. *ArchDaily*, https://www.archdaily.com/968905/architecting-the-metaverse.

Sung-mi, S. and Eun-seo, K. (2021, May 26). Metaverse Makes Digital Nomads the New Norm. *The Korea Economic Daily*, https://www.kedglobal.com/newsView/ked202105260007.

Sun-hwa, D. (2022, July 8). Forum Sheds Light on How Metaverse Can Reshape Entertainment Industry. *Korea Times*, https://www.koreatimes.co.kr/www/nation/2022/07/262_332369.html?fl.

Susskind, J. (2018). *Future Politics: Living Together in a World Transformed by Tech*. Oxford: Oxford University Press.

Szalai, G. (2021, April 7). Start-Up Backed by James Murdoch Launches AI Platform for Virtual Artists. *The Hollywood Reporter*, https://www.hollywoodreporter.com/business/business-news/authentic-artists-whose-investors-include-james-murdoch-launches-ai-platform-for-virtual-artists-4162497/.

Szulc, L. (2019). Profiles, Identities, Data: Making Abundant and Anchored Selves in a Platform Society. *Communication Theory*, 29, 257–276.

Takahashi, D. (2022, January 28). Emerge Brings Physical Touch to the Metaverse. *Venture Beat*, https://www.cnbc.com/2022/02/01/metaverse-real-estate-sales-top-500-million-metametric-solutions-says.html.

Terry, Q. and Keeny, S. (2022). *The Metaverse Handbook: Innovating for the Internet's Next Tectonic Shift*. Hoboken: Wiley.

The Economist. (2022, January 1). Virtual-Property Prices are Going Through the Roof, https://www.economist.com/business/2022/01/01/virtual-property-prices-are-going-through-the-roof.

Threekit. (n.d.). Virtual Products and NFTs in the Metaverse. https://www.threekit.com/how-to-sell-virtual-products-in-the-metaverse.

Tran, T. (2022, January 4). Facebook Hosted Three Huge Concerts in the Metaverse and They Seriously Flopped. *Futurism*, https://futurism.com/facebook-concert-metaverse-flopped.

Tremayne, T. and Gill, R. (2021, July 7). We Need to Kick Big Tech Out of the Metaverse. *Wired*, https://www.wired.co.uk/article/metaverse-big-tech.

Tsui, V. (2022, July 2). What Happens When Metaverse Meets Sports Leagues? *Jumpstart*, https://www.jumpstartmag.com/what-happens-when-metaverse-meets-sports-leagues/.

Uskali, T. and Ikonen, P. (2021). The Impact of Emotions on Immersive Journalism. In T. Uskali et al. (eds.) *Immersive Journalism as Storytelling: Ethics, Production, and Design* (pp. 49–59). London: Routledge.

Volpicelli, G. (2021). The Shapeshifting Cam Girl Rewriting the Rules of Digital Porn. *Wired*, https://www.wired.com/story/cam-girl-face-morph-digital-porn/.

Webster, A. (2021, November 1). The Metaverse, the Multiverse, and the End of Your Free Time. *The Verge*, https://www.theverge.com/22744724/metaverse-multiverse-entertainment-future-fortnite.

Wilser, J. (2022, March 8). Virtual Beers and Digital Orgasms: Welcome to the Age of Metaverse Commerce. *Coin Desk*, https://www.coindesk.com/layer2/2022/03/08/virtual-beers-and-digital-orgasms-welcome-to-the-age-of-metaverse-commerce/.

Wilson, J. (2022, May 11). The Overview: How Show Business Is Moving to the Metaverse. *Forbes*, https://www.forbes.com/sites/joshwilson/2022/05/11/the-overview-how-show-business-is-moving-to-the-metaverse/?sh=1f7d800b395d.

Winters, T. (2021). *The Metaverse: Prepare Now for the Next Big Thing!* Independently published.

Winterson, J. (2021). *12 Bytes: How We Got Here, Where We Might Go Next*. London: Jonathan Cape.

Zhou, M., Leenders, M. A. A. M. and Cong, L. M. (2018). Ownership in the Virtual World and the Implications for Long-Term User Innovation Success. *Technovation*, 78, 56–65.

Zuboff, S. (2019). *The Age of Surveillance Capitalism: The Fight for a Human Future at the New Frontier of Power*. London: Profile Books.

5 Law, Life, and Governance

The metaverse represents a further step in the interrelatedness of humans and technology. However, this is not a dyadic relationship as its environmental effects can only be ignored at everybody's peril. More broadly, this interrelatedness underscores a shift from an autonomous to a distributed self, best characterised as a matter of posthumanist embeddedness. The egalitarian ethics embedded in the posthumanist approach also serves as a tool for criticising what is seen as, essentially, a digital slave-owning society projected for the metaverse while also questioning the fundamental premises of modern society which imagines an independent human decision-maker at its core.

Given the transformative effect of the metaverse, matters of governance will also be of great importance. While there are important challenges (already familiar from today's internet) to metaverse governance, it should not be understood as anarchic or lawless. Instead, governance regimes will be set in the interactions (and power struggles) among states and platforms and mostly automated through digital architecture and AI tools. Finally, while distribution and tokenisation of governance are often presented as solutions to the problems inherent in both state and platform governance, it is argued in this chapter that they cause no fewer problems than they solve.

5.1 Conceptualising Life

The foreseeable impact of the metaverse cannot be fully appreciated without also considering its effects on the human self. Here, as in the preceding discussion, the metaverse is best understood less in terms of fundamental and seismic shifts and more as an intensification (and a logical step forward) of developments that are already evident today. In today's era of platforms and algorithmic governance, it is already the case that technologies are fundamentally interwoven with everyday activities, habits, movements, and living conditions (Chan 2022: 175). In fact, one can already observe a mutual

DOI: 10.4324/9781003355861-5

entanglement of humans and their technologies to the extent of being co-constituted and permanently malleable (see Kalpokas 2021). While Latour (2021: 29), for example, attributes the situation whereby 'we're not exactly old-fashioned "humans" anymore' to the post-lockdown condition, such hybridisation processes are older and more all-encompassing and can be traced to the overall technologisation of today's society.

Part of the drive for ever greater and more intense technologisation could be seen as commercial-technological, whereby increasing demand for data has led to technology having been embedded across multiple levels of human life – after all, as Couldry and Mejias (2019: xii) observe, '[t]echnologies work, and have consequences for human life, only by being woven into what people do, where they find meaning, and how their lives are interdependent'. In other words, there is no such thing as a separate existence of technology – or, at least, such existence does not make sense and leads to the corresponding technologies being discarded (just like it is impossible to imagine a human without their technological and natural habitat). Meanwhile, when entire domains of human action become inseparable from the corresponding technological infrastructures, one can speak of human–technology hybrids, be it a farmer with their ox and their plough (or, to give a more contemporary example, a farmer, their tractor, and their plough) or, for that matter, the authors of this book, word processing software (which they do not own but merely access on a subscription basis), an internet connection, the devices used for writing, cloud storage used for collaboration, etc.

In light of the above, when considered together, the summands of the metaverse, namely, humans, hardware, and virtual worlds, would constitute what Chalmers (2022: 108) calls 'Reality+': an extended physical–digital world seamlessly blended together. On the one hand, such an extension of reality might be considered a liberatory place where fantasy can be unleashed and 'life imitates art', allowing one to have limitless and unconstrained experiences (Kim 2022). On the other hand, it turns out, such human-centric fantasy can only be possible by ignoring the interdependence of humans, technologies, and the environment. In particular, the environmental cost of living out technology-enabled fantasies tends to be overlooked, ignoring the tremendous energy, resource, and raw material consumption that characterises digital technologies (see e.g. Crawford 2021; Brevini 2022). For this reason, a true picture of interconnectedness can only be appreciated when both animate and inanimate nature is added into the equation – after all, the farmer of the previous example is unimaginable without the land being ploughed and without hay for the ox (or fuel for the tractor and the emissions produced by that same tractor); likewise, the writing of this book would not have been possible without electricity (and the corresponding carbon footprint), the raw materials necessary for the devices used and the electronic waste into which the latter will one day turn, the environmental impact of the connectivity and cloud infrastructure, etc. Given the relatively low-tech nature of an endeavour like writing a book, and comparing that with the necessity to manufacture entirely new generations of headsets and haptic devices, largely rewire network infrastructure, provide the necessary storage capacity for a persistent 3D metaverse where every action is recorded and has effects, etc., the massive interrelatedness of the virtual self not just with technology but also with the natural environment becomes painfully clear.

Such interconnectedness also ought to be seen as a challenge to the modern idea of human agency and self-sufficiency that had been characteristic of Western philosophical thought at least since the Enlightenment, although its roots can also be traced to Renaissance humanism (see e.g. Kalpokas 2021). Crucially, a core tenet of modernity has been 'the participation of the self in creating knowledge about the self' as well the capacity for self-reflection and obtaining critical knowledge for the purpose of realising freedom-qua-autonomy; meanwhile, today, the capacity for knowledge generation and decision-making is anywhere in the continuum between being shared with and delegated to the digital infrastructure (Fisher 2022: 1). In fact, the very nature of knowledge and, correspondingly, agency based on that knowledge has changed: from that which has been processed by and through the self to the one which is processed by the algorithm (Fisher 2022: 2). Crucially, then, one ought to think in terms of reconstituting matters of action and agency as 'distributed between *people and things*' (Carter 2021: 211). In this way, as Neyland (2019: 11) puts it, daily life 'is an ongoing composition in which humans and non-humans participate'. Indeed, it must be admitted that 'the very cogito that Descartes rendered independent and pure is shaped by the objects and artifacts that surround it', which today include technological and virtual artefacts as well (Aydin 2021: 101).

Indeed, the nature of today's existence can be conceptualised in terms of 'assemblages of algorithms, platforms, and people' (Siles et al. 2019: 2; see also e.g. Lawtoo 2022: 89). Such assemblages are only going to expand significantly when one considers that in the metaverse humans will have to share their agency, in terms of technology alone, not just with algorithms, platforms, and their users but also with more or less autonomous non-human avatars and other kinds of bots, hardware, and AI-enabled tools involved in rendering the immersive 3D environments, haptics, and the connectivity infrastructure. Hence, one can observe a continuous trend of blurring of the distinction between reality and virtuality and between people, nature, and artefacts (The Onlife Initiative 2015: 44). In this way, a 'more-than-human' dimension is opened up, thereby emphasising the biology-transcending nature of today's life (Lupton 2020: 14). This, nevertheless, does not have to entail an oft-recurring fantasy of a technological upgrading of the human and, ultimately, merger with the machines – the latter still retains the anthropocentric desire for human primacy and improvement (for more on the difference, see e.g. Coeckelbergh 2020; Kalpokas 2021). Instead, it should be admitted that humans and their (technological and natural) environment are interwoven and co-constitutive, but without either having primacy (see e.g. Lupton 2020: 17; Miller 2020: 267).

The above position, broadly referred to as posthumanism, only logically follows its own assumptions when rejecting any claim of humans deserving preference over any other objects, both natural and artificial (Nath and Manna 2021: 2). Posthumanism, then, constitutes a break with the idea that humanity is somehow the centre of orientation and evaluation 'from which no judgment can escape, whether pertaining to science, philosophy, politics, or everyday practices' (Thomsen and Wamberg 2022: 1; see also Roden 2022: 81). Simultaneously, though, the egalitarianism inherent in posthumanist ethics precludes any other summand being brought up a hierarchical ladder – hence, decentring the human does not mean a simultaneous subjection to the machines. In short, any reductionist dichotomies of human vs technological (and, likewise, human vs natural or technological vs natural) agency fail to account for the shared nature of (inter)actions within hybrid physical–digital environments (Pentzhold and Bischof 2019: 7) and even more so in the digital-first environment of the metaverse. Instead, then, daily life and lived experience are best seen as 'an ongoing composition in which humans and non-humans participate' (Neyland 2019: 11), meaning that 'the individual is just one of the active decision-making agents' (Tulloch and Johnson 2022: 923). The metaverse, in addition, contributes a clearly identifiable visual layer to the decentring of the human self in the form of the avatar as a marked extension and part-externalisation of the self within a technologically curated environment.

The egalitarian posthumanist ethics also brings another set of considerations to light – namely, matters of behaviour in the metaverse. There are numerous problematic – and outright harmful – inter-human behaviours in the metaverse, some of which will be discussed in the next chapter. What attracts less attention, though, at least for now, is behaviour towards synthetic avatars. While, thus far, it has been treated in this book as a training ground for toxic inter-human relations, a posthumanist approach also sensitises us to the ethical issues pertaining to situations when synthetic humans are created, in the words of Hackl and Buzzell (2021: 137), for the purpose of 'automating satisfaction'. Indeed, many visions of the future, including those of the metaverse, feature what Ramirez (2021: 39) calls 'techno-republicanism': a substitution of the classical republican dogma that slavery is necessary to the flourishing of free humans by technologising the former. The metaverse as a fantasy space of self-realisation can seemingly only be fulfilled if one owns a workforce of 'digital humans' who will 'carry out tasks on our behalf, provide services to us, and curate our experiences with other people in the Metaverse' (Terry and Keeney 2022: 6). In this way, '[t]he techno-republican solution is slavery without slaves', supposedly doing away with racist and colonial practices; nevertheless, this newly found 'universality of the master' retains the same discriminatory framework of thought as past justifications of human slavery; the acceptance of techno-republicanism not only reproduces slave-owning practices in a new form but also, arguably, serves to at least partly redeem those of the past (Ramirez 2021: 42).

In one of the most troubling definitions, again provided by Terry and Keeney (2022: 8–9), such 'utility bots' would be 'AI-powered digital humans' who will 'inhabit our spaces, only if we invite them, of course, sitting idly in the background until we need them to carry out a task'. Such attitudes clearly exceed mere reproduction of racialised attitudes inherent in what Rottinghaus (2021) calls 'new white futurism' and, instead, amount to a whitewashing of the oppressive practices of the past while allowing for a replication of white colonist societies (even if they are virtual and populated by diverse avatars). However, this would likely not lead to egalitarianism among the biological humans either as one's success, productivity, and, therefore, capacity for engagement in metaversal leisure would depend on how many and how powerful digital slaves (understood as virtual productivity tools) one can afford. This also directly relates to the conflation of financial prowess with participation in governance through tokenisation, as discussed later in this chapter. Also, given the current prevalence of pretend-automation, whereby ostensibly AI-powered services are in reality outsourced to low-paid human workers in developing countries (as such substitution costs less and is easier to achieve than pure automation), there is no guarantee that what seems like technological slavery would not turn out to be human slavery redux.

On the other hand, the human–digital interaction is contradictory in itself. The relationship *is* reciprocal but in a specific way: digital agents can only be properly understood, in terms of their presence and placement, with regard to users and their data, while the users themselves, particularly in their avatar form (and, through it, in their physically grounded form), can only be realised in relation to the virtual objects they encounter. Simultaneously, the reliance on technological 'slaves' can be seen as outsourcing of action and decision-making to technological agents, which relegates humans to being passive participants in their own lives. After all, as Fisher (2022: 2) observes, the operation and legitimacy of modern institutions have been premised on the assumption of an independent decision-maker, capable of voting, signing contracts, making judgements of taste, and otherwise heavily involved in a range of life choices – all of which is put into question by the increasing role that algorithms, synthetic agents, and other digital artefacts play in daily life.

Moreover, one also has to consider the end goal – one's personal space in the metaverse is seen as a 'personal curated environment for productive digital work' (Terry and Keeney 2022: 9); here, one encounters, once again, the cult of productivity that paradoxically (given the emphasis on digital slavery) leads to self-exploitation – in other words, it is about having digital slaves to help increase the efficiency of one's own self-exploitation. Such permutations definitely touch upon, but also go beyond, the Hegelian master–slave dialectic, whereby the master, despite being in a nominally privileged position, is rendered contingent upon the slave for their status and existence. Where posthumanism goes beyond this dialectic is in its negation of a hierarchy in the first place, putting forth an ethical imperative to move away from dichotomies to interactions. By extension, then, the interactive relation between humans and digital agents should be one based on partnership, thus also precluding human self-exploitation.

In this way, the self shifts from an individual-autonomous to a relational one (Ess 2015: 89) or, rather, relational-many, as the idea of a single authoritative self becomes questionable through its extension via an avatar. Indeed, even the self as such should be re-rendered as a question. The metaverse may increase fluidity of the self: an avatar-centric existence would enable users to try out new identities to perhaps more closely resemble their own sense of the self than would be possible within their own physical bodies and/or within their offline social, cultural, or religious confines (Winters 2021: 21). After all, from a posthumanist standpoint, subjectivity is never a given but always performative, embedded in the current moment and the interactions therein (Roden 2022: 82). Existing research on games already suggests a broadening of the self through an 'avatar–player assemblage' and interactions with other such assemblages, i.e. other players (Wilde and Evans 2019: 802). Unsurprisingly, then, knowledge of oneself and others is 'always situated in the lively web of interdependencies' (Cielemęcka and Daigle 2019: 81). Indeed, establishing a separation between the physical individual and their avatar (or, even worse, considering the avatar to be 'fake' in the usual sense of the term) would be a mistake – the two are integrated into one another, with the avatar helping the individual transcend their bodily capacities and even the laws of physics (Golf-Pape et al. 2022). The metaverse would likely offer a suspension of the self in a way that is reminiscent of that present in today's games – 'a dynamic between the actual experience of playing here-and-now and the desired future not yet realized state' (Larsen and Walther 2020: 622). The result would, therefore, be an environment of continuous becoming, a 'temporal present' (Coleman 2018: 68).

There is, however, also a broader conceptual issue at stake here, and one strongly pertinent to the metaverse: the makeup of the social world. While, for Fisher (2022: 43), the rise in prominence of algorithmic judgement signals a move '[t]oward a post-social conception of the individual', this only holds for as long as *purely human* sociality is concerned. In the metaverse, however, such an assumption would be problematic by default: even speaking of humans narrowly conceived, the way their avatars are generated and displayed, the ways in which their interactions with other human avatars are managed, the way in which virtual environments are being rendered, etc. all have an impact on how sociality (and even one's experience of the self as an individual-qua-avatar and as a social agent) takes shape, meaning that sociality is at the very least 'impurely' human. Nevertheless, should one add synthetic actors, from virtual assistants and non-player characters to fully autonomous AI-powered avatars, into the mix, instead of entering some kind of post-social era, one would more likely be partaking in a novel – posthuman – kind of sociality.

Understanding the goings-on of the above form of sociality necessitates delving more deeply into posthumanist thought. Of note here is the posthumanist emphasis on relationality: as, for example, Braidotti (2019: 45–47) observes, '[w]e are relational beings, defined by the capacity to affect and be affected' and, therefore, 'flowing in a web of relations with human and non-human others'. The interrelatedness in question would, in all likelihood, come about by way of affect. As Seigworth and Gregg (2010: 1) rather cryptically put it, affect is about the passage of intensities 'that pass body to body (human, non-human, part-body and otherwise)' as well as 'in those resonances that circulate about, between and sometimes stick to bodies and worlds'. To put it differently, affect is a precognitive reaction that drives everything from instinctive responses to tapping of the foot when listening to music; it is also about the passing of emotions from person to person and emotional reactions to environmental changes (see, generally, Papacharissi 2016; Damasio 2018). Indeed, then, interactivity and relationality pertain not just to the self but to one's environment as well, with the latter becoming 'increasingly reactive as a result of the intricate mix between offline and online universes' (Dewandre 2020: 3). Thereby, offline data of an individual's gestures, emotions, and movements informs the avatar and its online surroundings just like the online data of the user's previous interactions affects the emotions, reactions, feelings, and behaviours of the physical human.

Effectively, then, the very distinction between the physical and the digital is losing importance in the first place – they simply become impossible to separate in most everyday situations and activities (Susskind 2018: 97). This clearly applies to feelings and emotions that would arise not from technology as an extrinsic cause but, instead, from the very interaction between humans and technologies – a matter of joint becoming (Tucker 2018: 39). However, this goes beyond perceptions and feelings, moving into everyday objects and other material aspects of a person's existence as well. In this context, fashion and accessories have proved perhaps the first harbinger of things to come, with styles and aesthetics moving freely between the virtual and the physical (see e.g. Maguire 2022). Such trends can only be expected to continue, signalling a self that transcends the physical and the virtual.

Of course, much of the metaverse still remains about potential yet to be realised, not least because the necessary technological solutions are not yet available, meaning that a fully-fledged metaverse – and, therefore, the physical-virtual self – would only gradually come about during the next several decades (Bradshaw 2022). Nevertheless, it is already evident that, as the metaverse expands to encompass an ever-growing set of activities, and as its use becomes ever more intertwined with core activities, such as socialisation, work, leisure, intimate relationships, etc., it will be not just inseparable from real life – it will, instead, become *the* real life as such, operating in the background and structuring daily existence through its coded architecture – the ultimate domain of power (Zickgraf 2021). It is, therefore, unsurprising that the companies currently investing in the metaverse are actively trying to position themselves at the heart of the entire technology stack, including code and design, data centres, hardware, and the AI to run it all (Adebayo 2022).

5.2 Conceptualising Governance

While even as of now, it must be admitted that 'Internet governance is a complicated mess' (Van Puyvelde and Brantly 2019: 55), the development of the metaverse is only going to complicate matters even further, particularly when virtual behaviours go awry. Crucially, though, as with many things pertaining to the metaverse, there may be somewhat less novelty than the hype surrounding the idea suggests. After all, the challenges inherent in the governance of online environments are well known and have already been extensively covered back when 'cyber', rather than 'meta', was *the* fashionable prefix (see, perhaps most notably, Johnson and Post 1996). In brief, the online environment, in either incarnation, undermines the customary connection between geography on the one hand and the government power of control, user behaviours and effects, legitimacy of regulatory policies, and the territorial extent of the application of laws on the other (Murray 2019: 17). It is already a well-known challenge that, while 'policing has historically followed the organization of political, social and economic life within national territories', owing to the internet being global, online threats are 'an inherently de-territorialized phenomenon', thus creating a mismatch that both political and law enforcement bodies find difficult to overcome (Yar and Steinmetz 2019: 16). Additional complexity is added by the ease and speed of global data and content transfers, putting further pressure on politicians, courts, and law enforcement agencies (Murray 2019: 14).

While there is a rich tradition of thinking and behaving online as if traditional laws did not apply (think of Barlow's *Declaration of Independence of Cyberspace* as a – relatively – early proclamation to that effect), state and court practice has since demonstrated on multiple occasions that the actual governance landscape is significantly more complicated and nuanced (Rizzo 2022). Both democratic states (the US and the UK, for example) and non-democratic ones (China and Russia in particular), as well as regional organisations (the EU being a prominent example), have used their legislative power to regulate in areas ranging from individual and national security to commerce. However, it is also true that, more than in any other domain, states are far from the sole – or main – shapers of regulatory matters and enforcers thereof – the famous state monopoly of control, had it ever existed beyond ideal type, has certainly been broken. After all, as Moynihan, Buchser and Wallace (2022) observe, one of the greatest challenges of today is that the framing of metaverse governance 'is being entirely led by commercial interests', meaning that '[t]here is very little public debate about how our future digital environment should look, who should design it, what its purpose should be and what standards should govern its operation'. It is thus likely that, by the time other actors (states, civil society organisations, etc.) join in, standards would already be set and, therefore, difficult to change, even if they are deemed to be societally or politically suboptimal or completely undesirable.

Still, governments such as the Chinese will undoubtedly aim to have a strong grip over what happens in the metaverse and what their citizens do there, engaging in censorship along the way (Kharpal 2022). And, given the increasingly tight grip that the state has on the technology sector there, the balance of power in enforcing regulation would be completely different in China compared with the West. That, in turn, might lead to the splintering (Balkanisation) of the metaverse. While similar warnings have already been voiced with regard to the current internet concerning the divergences in regulation, for example, among the US, the EU, China, and Russia, given that the metaverse would exceed the current internet in its scope and impact on daily life (perhaps becoming *the* locus of daily life in an immersive way), regulatory divergence would be much more strongly felt not just by businesses (that now have perhaps the clearest sense of differences, for example, in dealing with different privacy laws and other regulatory requirements) but also by individual users. Even across the West, the metaverse should not be seen as lawless and starting from a blank regulatory slate – instead, as is the case with search, social media, and other equally global spheres today, platform companies will have to abide by the laws of their states of incorporation, even if the existing laws would not initially be tailored for this new domain (Abraham 2022). The implication, then, is that laws pertaining to technologies should be formulated broadly enough to be future-proofed (Holt, Bossler and Seigfried-Spellar 2022: 693). A key obstacle, however, tends to be an inertia in legal and policy thought whereby today's legal systems still typically presume a physical world by default, which is in sharp contrast to the convergence (i.e. the process of bringing everything into the digital domain) that is taking place in the real world (Murray 2019: 13–14).

Even some metaverse enthusiasts are calling for greater state involvement in metaverse regulation to ensure that rules, standards, and regulations are equitable, thus also rather explicitly acknowledging the likely failure of complete industry self-regulation (see, notably, Ball 2022: 299–300). While the involvement of states and regional organisations (such as the EU) is, in all likelihood, unavoidable, it will nevertheless raise issues similar to the regulation of the current internet, including, in addition to Balkanisation, regulatory lag, whereby states can only regulate current and past issues, meaning that, by the time regulation is agreed upon, it might be already outdated, and there will be a lack of capacity to enforce existing regulations and limited legitimacy of the rules and regulations that have been passed. Here, the matter of lag (and, more broadly, lawmaker competence) looms particularly large: as lawmakers face a knowledge deficit in comparison with technology entrepreneurs, the law typically fails to anticipate change or contains loopholes allowing societally undesirable platform company practices to continue (Moynihan, Buchser and Wallace 2022). Also, the extent to which such regulation is feasible, at least in democratic societies, is unclear, given political priorities, lobbying, civil society pressure, etc. Others, meanwhile, are calling on states and the civil society to step in and develop regulatory and ethical frameworks for the metaverse before industry self-regulation and standards kick in, citing what is seen as the generally self-serving nature of current corporate-first AI ethics (see e.g. Entsminger, Esposito and Tse 2022).

Focus is thus often on finding the balance between legislating to protect fundamental rights and freedoms from self-serving platform policies and avoiding regulatory overreach so that the actions of governments do not become a threat by themselves (Moynihan, Buchser and Wallace 2022). Nevertheless, until effective domestic and international frameworks are developed (if at all), platform companies transpire to be the only actors capable of actually bringing about and enacting norms (Holt, Bossler and Seigfried-Spellar 2022: 693; see also Abraham 2022). However, such private regulation would almost unavoidably be tainted by commercial interests or at least suspicions thereof, thereby creating legitimacy issues no lesser than those faced by states (although platform companies would still be significantly more effective in enforcement through their algorithmic governance capacities – see, generally, Kalpokas 2019).

Transnational cooperation is certainly necessary owing to the global nature of the metaverse but also for liberal democracies to be able to shape standards with regard to the issues of privacy, transparency, and respect for human rights more generally (Moynihan, Buchser and Wallace 2022). Nevertheless, for a global framework to be effective, it would necessitate cooperation between not just democracies but also authoritarian states – and, as attempts at cyberspace governance to date demonstrate, such cooperation is hard to achieve. Moreover, interpretations as to appropriate governance differ even among liberal democracies as well – consider, for example, an increasingly prescriptive stance taken by the EU and a significantly more hands-off approach (except for matters of national security) adopted by the US. Likewise, even in cases of overarching similarity, differences in wording and emphasis may prove to be an impediment to effective collaboration (Holt, Bossler and Seigfried-Spellar 2022: 51–52; see also Yar and Steinmetz 2019: 18).

Crucially, then, the metaverse should be seen not as a completely separate domain in terms of its governance but as an intersection of (and often tension between) corporate and state power (Lambach 2019: 18). Such an uneasy relationship is not unlike the current state of internet governance. Also, not unlike the current state of governance, even in absence of a unitary global framework for overarching matters, sector-specific issues and smaller-scale matters of everyday interactions, behavioural norms, and technological standards will most likely be dealt with by the industry actors themselves and coalitions thereof. Hence, most interactions on metaverse platforms will take place in accordance with private or sector-specific rules and regulations that will have significant impact on the daily lives of users – and, in the case of concentration of the user base within several very large platforms, it is not inconceivable that their influence over individuals would rival that of states (Abraham 2022).

There is also an important practical shift that has been present across online platforms and various instances of automated smart governance initiatives and tools: a 'shift from law enforced by *people* to law enforced by *technology*', whereby rules (including laws) are being upheld not by a threat of sanction but by the removal of the very possibility of non-compliance (Susskind 2018: 105). There are, of course, different degrees of removal, with automobile speed control being a good example: from completely driver-controlled speed to introduction of systems that make speeding as difficult as possible (see e.g. Posky 2022; Stumpf 2022) to, with the advent of autonomous vehicles, the elimination of the possibility of speeding altogether as the vehicle would dynamically adjust to speed limits, with the driver out of the loop. This points towards an increasing growth in algorithmic regulation, whereby '*thousands upon thousands* of decisions [...] will be taken every day, decided automatically and executed seamlessly with no right of appeal' (Susskind 2018: 191). Indeed, the scope of the metaverse, the sheer amount and variety of content, from games and experiences to everyday interactions among avatars, and the sensitivity of such content (few would agree with human moderators parsing through conversations on the metaverse) make AI-enabled moderation an easy-to-sell option. Moreover, that would be strongly in line with what Fisher (2022) sees as an overall trend of discarding human subjectivity and decision-making capacity in favour of their allegedly more objective algorithmic counterpart.

Nevertheless, automated governance would not be a silver bullet either: first of all, such content moderation necessitates significant amounts of data to be trained upon and to subsequently operate, which, instead of alleviating privacy concerns, simply raises new ones; secondly, one cannot avoid the same set of concerns that already plague content moderation on social media: the mismatch between commercial and public interests (Elkin-Korel 2020: 6). Likewise, in an even deeper sense than today's social media, this would put platforms at the forefront of decisions concerning free speech and acceptable human behaviour – matters that, until recently, were the domain of legal norms and judicial decision-making; unlike traditional forms of regulation, corporate decision-making typically lacks transparency and an effective appeals procedure (Elkin-Korel 2020: 6).

While it is beyond the scope of this book to delve into the mythology of algorithmic governance (for that, see e.g. Kalpokas 2019), it can be summarised that the ideal type would be run by machine learning algorithms that are smart and adaptive and act promptly to remove any potential threats or to nudge users towards behavioural change – all this without any human judgement involved (Murray 2019: 81). In practice, though, such optimistic accounts fail to account for the biases still inherent in algorithmic governance tools or for the ways humans continue to be involved in setting and vetting algorithmic governance techniques (see e.g. Issar and Aneesh 2022; Kordzadeh and Ghasemaghaei 2022). Here, again, the impact of any biases and misapplications of such tools is going to have a significantly more noticeable effect courtesy of the scope and impact of the metaverse as an immersive version of daily life. However, given the fact that discussions of algorithmic governance and bias remain a rather niche subject necessitating greater public awareness and civil society involvement, there would likely be limited contestation and scrutiny of such techniques. Also, this signals an unavoidable gap between the promotional imagery of metaversal creativity, freedom, fantasy, and play on the one hand and data-based personalisation and encoded governance on the other.

As an alternative to both platform power and greater state involvement, metaverse enthusiasts typically propose the idea of decentralised autonomous organisations (DAOs): in such organisations, rules would be set by the members themselves (e.g. through a vote) and automatically written into the code that underpins the organisation's architecture, thereby precluding the need for a central authority (see e.g. Winters 2021: 43). Based on blockchain technology, in theory at least, such organisations would provide an incontestable record of any governance arrangements while allowing all members of the organisation to participate in proportion to the share of tokens held – all without a central authority. Such decentralisation, coupled with the dominance of user-generated content, proponents claim, could be seen as a development that 'shifts power away from platforms towards creators' (Clark 2022). However, important caveats are overlooked in such accounts.

Indeed, it is overly optimistic to view DAOs and the growing reliance on blockchain as paragons of democracy. On platforms that allow the purchase of virtual land to acquire digital 'citizenship', given the price and exclusivity of such ownership, the system of governance that ensues would be more akin to oligarchy or, at best, a democracy of the landed gentry, similar to that which existed in Britain until the second half of the 19th century (see e.g. Thompson 2019). The proliferation of the ability to purchase tokens that give a corresponding share in the decision-making of digital ventures and, in some cases, also offline enterprises (as touted by e.g. Hackl, Lueth and Di Bartolo 2022: 12–13) only further reinforces the 'money-equals-power' interpretation of the alleged democracy in tokenised governance. Simultaneously, though, the design of such strategy posits empowerment as a side effect at best: the real purpose, as formulated by Hackl, Lueth and Di Bartolo (2022: 13) is that '[t]his is a great way to create a sticky user-base that is willing to open their crypto wallets because they help shape the ecosystem'. To translate from industry parlance, this strategy helps to lock users in as the sunken costs of their ambition to purchase influence accumulate; moreover, users' sunken costs simultaneously represent income for the venture, thus creating a win–win situation for the latter's masterminds. Indeed, as Hackl, Lueth and Di Bartolo (2022: 91) rather openly observe, if one is able to combine the fulfilment of a social or personal need (something that platforms already do) and tokenisation, the result is 'a deeper reward system than anything we've seen before on the Internet'. In this way, DAOs may be further removed from user empowerment than otherwise thought.

Of course, there is also another strategy, whereby individuals do not have to buy into governance but are rewarded with tokens for their contribution – for example, performing tasks that would usually be paid for (see e.g. Terry and Keeney 2022: 25). And here, precisely, is the flip side for the user: while in the above scenario the founders benefit from monetising the desire for power and influence, here they deprive users of monetisation of their efforts by awarding vanity tokens of uncertain (and often no) value. While such tokens may carry some perks, such as a right to vote on decisions concerning the future direction of the app itself (the sine qua non of DAOs), the share of the vote for each contributor is likely to be minuscule, unless they can hijack the process by e.g. affording to dedicate significant amounts of computational power or outsource contributions to microtaskers in developing countries while reaping the rewards (similar instances are common in e.g. cryptocurrency mining). This, however, would certainly amount to something completely different than democratisation of governance – instead, the ability to buy into governance would be reinforced.

The challenges, however, do not end here: while decentralised token-based apps look good in theory, they are fully dependent on the hype created around them in order to keep user contributions flowing; decentralisation only works if there is a constant increase in user-contributors: increasing amounts of users necessitate an increasing amount of resources, which means that existing users need to attract more users in order to keep the platform going, etc. (this, albeit with a highly positive spin, is described by e.g. Terry and Keeney 2022: 24–25). Seen in this light, decentralised apps have the basic structure of a Ponzi scheme. If, for whatever reason, the app started haemorrhaging users with at least above-average contributions, the entire edifice would quickly crumble, taking away user contributions in time, effort, and computational resources (and, if there had been an ability to purchase tokens, also money). For the founders, on the contrary, this is a relatively risk-free option as all the resources necessary to scale up the venture (up to the electricity costs necessary to keep the service running) had been provided by the users themselves in exchange for vanity tokens that later turned out to be worthless. The same amounts to tokenised crowdsourcing (see e.g. Terry and Keeney 2022: 34–35): while such tokens are often (mis)sold as investment opportunities, this puts individuals in financial risk that can only be mitigated by bringing in an ever-larger number of new contributors – again, Ponzi-style.

Greater reliance on DAOs, and blockchain more generally, also tends to be seen as a straight pathway towards an interoperable metaverse. Nevertheless, such interoperability might be more difficult to achieve than most of its proponents allege because it involves overcoming not just corporate decision-making logics but also a plethora of technical challenges. Moreover, bringing any assets across platform boundaries may cause issues pertaining to gameplay quality, rendering, immersion, or perhaps even rule-breaking – even though technically and format-wise such integration might be possible (Hackl, Lueth and Di Bartolo 2022: 18–22). This is also on top of the different aesthetics and functionalities (how would a banana skin or an octopus avatar perform in a football simulator?), different ways of rendering (e.g. is a face a single item or a collection of multiple separately rendered items?), record storage and sharing, etc. (see, most notably, Ball 2022). Notably, Ball (2022: 43–44) provides perhaps the most user-friendly account of the difficulties involved: there are issues that are impossible to overcome unless specially designed for (just like in the physical world, while you can bring any item to Venus, it would be immediately crushed unless specifically designed), there are issues of practicality (farming on the Moon might theoretically be possible, but the need to build large-scale climate-controlled environments renders it impractical – at least for the foreseeable future), and then there are issues of artificial boundaries (for example, most items can be brought to most places on Earth, but there are political, economic, social, cultural, and other obstacles to doing so). And, while the interoperability optimists would foresee consumer pressure for platforms to ensure the transferability of assets, credentials, etc., especially citing real-world analogies of possessions and identities that can be easily carried on one's person (see e.g. Hackl, Lueth and Di Bartolo 2022: 22), that would only work *unless* platform silos provided their users with all they need, with the people they need – and precisely that seems to be on the agenda for most of the current platform companies bent on dominating the metaverse, from Meta to Epic Games (*Fortnite*).

No less importantly, the various physical world analogies are imperfect since the physical world exists independently of humans and did not have to be produced by humans *ex nihilo* (whether one believes this heavy lifting to have been performed by nature, a divine entity, or a 'spaghetti monster' does not really matter here). However, when human production is concerned, siloisation prevails, be it socio-political (from clans and tribes to states) or economic (including entities as diverse as medieval guilds or current companies and, indeed, platforms). Ball (2022: 58–59), meanwhile, provides a slightly different false analogy by framing citizens as somehow completely separate from states: according to him, just as individuals have built the physical world independently of their states, the virtual one will be independent of platform companies. However, this analogy completely misses the regulatory, identitarian, economic, security, etc. role of states as well as their capacity to establish and maintain borders for both people and goods. Hence, while it might be true that the individuals have built the human layer of the world (which is certainly not all something to be proud of), they have mostly done so under the conditions of their states' choosing. Moreover, because of collective action problems, citizens often fail to act on high-stake issues *precisely* where state is slow to regulate, with climate change mitigation being a prominent example.

Likewise, even some of those who are otherwise enthusiastic about the interoperable metaverse recognise important differences between the development of open internet standards and the present condition in which the metaverse takes shape: instead of the non-profit origins of the internet, the metaverse is being developed from scratch by private profit-seeking businesses 'for the explicit purpose of commerce, data collection, advertising, and the sale of virtual products', while online platforms are already holding great sway over their users' lives and are now integrated across multiple sectors (Ball 2022: 16). Also, the assertion that users would necessarily *want* to carry all of their belongings and data with them and, consequently, push for interoperability remains exactly that – an assertion. It does not take into account the possibility of users wanting to maintain e.g. separate professional and private identities (and thus also needing different assets) or maintaining separate identities as a way to resist datafication or to protect their privacy for various reasons, from political to sexual. Indeed, particularly the intention to protect one's privacy would find validation in the current corporate promotional literature on the metaverse (see e.g. Hackl, Lueth and Di Bartolo 2022) whereby interoperability and the resulting user transparency mean that *the whole* (and not just platform-specific) user data can be obtained and used to produce insights.

In all likelihood, then, it will be the choices of the architects of specific 'sociotechnical assemblages' (Burke 2019: 12) – platforms – that are going to shape how the world is lived and experienced – the possibilities and impossibilities that determine behaviours and underlying considerations. Even the decision to confer a certain amount of decision-making functions to a certain group of users (if at all) is something to be made at a corporate level in light of the adopted business model. That in itself goes at least partly against the decentralisation and empowerment thesis prominent among metaverse optimists. Ultimately, those platform-level decisions, built into their digital architectures, end up 'affecting institutions, economic transactions, and social and cultural practices – hence, forcing governments and states to adjust their legal and democratic structures' (van Dijck, Poell and de Waal 2018: 2). It must, therefore, be acknowledged that the social is not merely reflected by the platforms but *produced* instead, reflecting the specific values and priorities inherent in platform business models (van Dijck, Poell and de Waal 2018: 2–3) and even more so in the case of metaverse platforms owing to the breadth and immersiveness of the latter.

The ever-more pervasive nature of datafication, unavoidable owing to the technological needs of the metaverse, will also contribute to new, more effective, modalities of platform governance – the more is known about the society and the individuals that compose it, the easier it becomes to 'intervene and manipulate these processes in accordance with particular aims' (Krasmann 2020: 2099). After all, reliance on the predictive promise of algorithms to serve users content that they are deemed to like or that is expected to nudge them towards a desired behaviour (e.g. purchase of a sponsored item or service) effectively closes the future's open horizon by essentially causing what had only been a prediction by way of foreclosing alternative options (Nowotny 2022: 50–51). Such a tendency would be particularly acute in the metaverse owing to the malleability of the entirety of its environment. Hence, while, on the one hand, the desire to escape reality, its troubles, and discomforts could be one of the driving forces behind the adoption of digital technologies (see e.g. Han, Bergs and Moorhouse 2022), such an escape does not automatically lead towards a utopia of liberation.

As should be clear from the preceding, the struggles for metaverse governance will involve especially high stakes. That is because the decisions on governance models and tools will be highly consequential for the everyday lives of metaverse users and the ways they go about almost every aspect of their daily routines. At the moment, a platformisation (and, therefore, further extension of private governance) scenario with limited inter-platform interoperability seems to be the most likely one, with states probably continuing to exert influence on overarching matters (such as data protection). That is unless significant user pressure forces alternative models to be brought about – although, at the moment, there are few indications such pressure would be likely to occur.

Bibliography

Abraham, A. (2022, April 4). Law & Order in the Metaverse. *FinExtra*, https://www.finextra.com/the-long-read/376/law--order-in-the-metaverse.

Adebayo, K. S. (2022, March 2). Meta Describes How AI will Unlock the Metaverse. *VentureBeat*, https://venturebeat.com/2022/03/02/meta-describes-how-ai-will-unlock-the-metaverse/.

Aydin, C. (2021). *Extimate Technology: Self-Formation in a Technological World*. London: Routledge.

Ball, M. (2022). *The Metaverse and How It Will Revolutionize Everything*. New York: W. W. Norton & Company.

Bradshaw, T. (2022, April 4). Virtual Worlds Are Still More Minecraft than Metaverse. *Financial Times*, https://www.ft.com/content/030f55f4-0b95-4e89-a903-6b9a48070f4c.

Braidotti, R. (2019). *Posthuman Knowledge*. Cambridge: Polity.

Brevini, B. (2022). *Is AI Good for the Planet?* Cambridge: Polity.

Burke, A, (2019). Occluded Algorithms. *Big Data & Society*, doi: 10.1177/2053951719858743.

Carter, S. (2021). Semi-Autonomous Digital Objects: Between Humans and Machines. In J. Perriam and S. Carter (eds.) *Understanding Digital Societies* (pp. 195–221). Los Angeles: SAGE.

Chalmers, D. J. (2022). *Reality +: Virtual Worlds and the Problems of Philosophy*. New York: W. W. Norton & Company.

Chan, M. (2022). *Digital Reality: The Body and Digital Technologies*. New York: Bloomsbury Academic.

Cielemęcka, O. and Daigle, C. (2019). Posthuman Sustainability: An Ethos for our Anthropocentric Future. *Theory, Culture & Society*, 36(7–8), 67–87.

Clark, K. (2022, January 20). The Metaverse Data Privacy Debate Is Getting Feisty: Here's what You Need to Know. *The Drum*, https://www.thedrum.com/news/2022/01/20/the-metaverse-data-privacy-debate-getting-feisty-here-s-what-you-need-know.

Coeckelbergh, M. (2020). *AI Ethics*. Cambridge: The MIT Press.

Coleman, R. (2018). Social Media and the Materialisation of the Affective Present. In T. D. Sampson, S. Maddison and D. Ellis (eds.) *Affect and Social Media: Emotion, Mediation, Anxiety and Contagion* (pp. 67–75). London: Rowman & Littlefield.

Couldry, N. and Mejias, U. A. (2019). *The Costs of Connection: How Data Is Colonizing Human Life and Appropriating It for Capitalism*. Stanford: Stanford University Press.

Crawford, K. (2021). *Atlas of AI: Power, Politics, and the Planetary Costs of Artificial Intelligence*. New Haven: Yale University Press.

Damasio, A. (2018). *The Strange Order of Things: Life, Feeling, and the Making of Cultures*. New York: Pantheon Books.

Dewandre, N. (2020). Big Data: From Modern Fears to Enlightened and Vigilant Embrace of New Beginnings. *Big Data & Society*, doi: 10.1177/2053951720936708.

Elkin-Korel, N. (2020). Contesting Algorithms: Restoring the Public Interest in Content Filtering by Artificial Intelligence. *Big Data & Society*, doi: 10.1177/2053951720932296.

Entsminger, J., Esposito, M. and Tse, T. (2022, August 17). Who Will Establish Metaverse Ethics? *Project Syndicate*, https://www.project-syndicate.org/commentary/who-establishes-metaverse-ethics-by-josh-entsminger-et-al-2022-08.

Ess, C. (2015). The Onlife Manifesto: Philosophical Backgrounds, Media Usages, and the Futures of Democracy and Equality. In L. Floridi (ed.) *The Onlife Manifesto: Being Human in a Hyperconnected Era* (pp. 89–109). Cham: Springer.

Fisher, E. (2022). *Algorithms and Subjectivity: The Subversion of Critical Knowledge*. London: Routledge.

Golf-Pape, M. et al. (2022). Embracing Falsity Through the Metaverse: The Case of Synthetic Customer Experiences. *Business Horizons*, doi: 10.1016/j.bushor.2022.07.007.

Hackl, C. and Buzzell, J. (2021). *The Augmented Workforce* (2nd ed.). North Kansas City: Renown Publishing.

Hackl, C., Lueth, D. and Di Bartolo, T. (2022). *Navigating the Metaverse: A Guide to Limitless Possibilities in a Web 3.0 World*. Hoboken: Wiley.

Han, D. D., Bergs, Y. and Moorhouse, N. (2022). Virtual Reality Consumer Experience Escapes: Preparing for the Metaverse. *Virtual Reality*, doi: 10.1007/s10055-022-00641-7.

Holt, T. J., Bossler, A. M. and Seigfried-Spellar, K. C. (2022). *Cybercrime and Digital Forensics: An Introduction* (3rd ed.). London: Routledge.

Issar, S. and Aneesh, A. (2022). What is Algorithmic Governance? *Sociology Compass*, 16, 1–14.

Johnson, D. and Post, D. (1996). Law and Borders: The Rise of Law in Cyberspace. *Stanford Law Review*, 48(5), 1367–1402.

Kalpokas, I. (2019). *Algorithmic Governance: Politics and Law in the Post-Human Era*. London: Palgrave Macmillan.

Kalpokas, I. (2021). *Malleable, Digital, and Posthuman: A Permanently Beta Life*. Bingley: Emerald.

Kharpal, A. (2022, February 14). China's Tech Giants Push Toward an $8 Trillion Metaverse Opportunity – One that will Be Highly Regulated. *CNBC*, https://www.cnbc.com/2022/02/14/china-metaverse-tech-giants-latest-moves-regulatory-action.html.

Kim, K. (2022, June 16). In the Metaverse, Life Imitates Art. *The New Yok Times*, https://www.nytimes.com/2022/06/16/special-series/krista-kim-metaverse-nft-art-reality.html.

Kordzadeh, N. and Ghasemaghaei, M. (2022). Algorithmic Bias: Review, Synthesis, and Future Research Directions. *European Journal of Information Systems*, 31(3), 388–409.

Krasmann, S. (2020). The Logic of the Surface: On the Epistemology of Algorithms in Times of Big Data. *Information, Communication & Society*, 23(14), 2096–2109.

Lambach, D. (2019). The Territorialization of Cyberspace. *International Studies Review*, doi: https://doi.org/10.1093/isr/viz022.

Larsen, L. J. and Walther, B. K. (2020). The Ontology of Gameplay: Toward a New Theory. *Games and Culture*, 15(6), 609–931.

Latour, B. (2021). *After Lockdown: A Metamorphosis*. Cambridge: Polity Press.

Lawtoo, N. (2022). Posthumanism and Mimesis: An Introduction. *Journal of Posthumanism*, 2(2), 87–100.

Lupton, D. (2020). *Data Selves*. Cambridge: Polity.

Maguire, L. (2022, April 12). Is the Metaverse Influencing Real-Life Trends? *Vogue Business*, https://www.voguebusiness.com/technology/is-the-metaverse-influencing-real-life-trends.

Miller, V. (2020). *Understanding Digital Culture* (2nd ed.). Los Angeles: SAGE.

Moynihan, H., Buchser, M. and Wallace, J. (2022, April 25). What is the Metaverse? *Chatham House*, https://www.chathamhouse.org/2022/04/what-metaverse.

Murray, A. (2019). *Information Technology Law: The Law & Society*. Oxford: Oxford University Press.

Nath, R. and Manna, R. (2021). From Posthumanism to Ethics of Artificial Intelligence. *AI & Society*, doi: 10.1007/s00146-021-01274-1.

Neyland, D. (2019). *The Everyday Life of an Algorithm*. London: Palgrave Macmillan.

Nowotny, H. (2022). *In AI We Trust: Power, Illusion and Control of Predictive Algorithms*. Cambridge: Polity Press.

Papacharissi, Z. (2016). *Affective Publics: Sentiment, Technology, and Politics*. Oxford: Oxford University Press.

Pentzhold, C. and Bischof, A. (2019). Making Affordances Real: Socio-Material Prefiguration, Performed Agency, and Coordinated Activities in Human-Robot Communication. *Social Media + Society*, doi: 10.1177/2056305119865472.

Posky, M. (2022, July 12). Europe Now Requires Speed Regulators for All New Vehicles. *The Truth about Cars*, https://www.thetruthaboutcars.com/2022/07/europe-now-requires-speed-regulators-for-all-new-vehicles/.

Ramirez, J. J. (2021). *Against Automation Mythologies: Business Science Fiction and the Ruse of Robotics*. London: Routledge.

Rizzo, J. (2022, April 3). The Future of NFTs Lies with the Courts. *Wired*, https://www.wired.com/story/nfts-cryptocurrency-law-copyright/.

Roden, D. (2022). Posthumanism: Critical, Speculative, Biomorphic. In M. R. Thomsen and J. Wamberg (eds.) *The Bloomsbury Handbook of Posthumanism* (pp. 81–93). New York: Bloomsbury Academic.

Rottinghaus, A. R. (2021). Smart Homes and the New White Futurism. *Journal of Futures Studies*, 25(4), 45–56.

Seigworth, G. J. and Gregg, M. (2010). An Inventory of Shimmers. In M. Gregg and G. J. Seigworth (eds.) *The Affect Theory Reader* (pp. 1–26). Durham: Duke University Press.

Siles, I. et al. (2019). The Mutual Domestication of Users and Algorithmic Recommendation on Netflix. *Communication, Culture & Critique*, doi: 10.1093/ccc/tcz025.

Stumpf, R. (2022, July 6). Europe Now Requires All New Cars to Have Anti-Speeding Monitors. *The Drive*, https://www.thedrive.com/news/europe-now-requires-all-new-cars-to-have-anti-speeding-monitors.

Susskind, J. (2018). *Future Politics: Living Together in a World Transformed by Tech*. Oxford: Oxford University Press.

Terry, Q. and Keeney, S. (2022). *The Metaverse Handbook: Innovating for the Internet's Next Tectonic Shift*. Hoboken: Wiley.

The Onlife Initiative. (2015). Background Document: Rethinking Public Spaces in the Digital Transition. In L. Floridi (ed.) *The Onlife Manifesto: Being Human in a Hyperconnected Era* (pp. 41–47). Cham: Springer.

Thompson, F. M. L. (2019). Britain. In D. Spring (ed.) *European Landed Elites in the Nineteenth Century* (pp. 22–44). Baltimore: Johns Hopkins University Press.

Thomsen, M. R. and Wamberg, J. (2022). Introduction. In M. R. Thomsen and J. Wamberg (eds.) *The Bloomsbury Handbook of Posthumanism* (pp. 1–10). New York: Bloomsbury Academic.

Tucker, I. (2018). Digitally Mediated Emotion: Simondon, Affectivity and Individuation. In T. D. Sampson, S. Maddison and D. Ellis (eds.) *Affect and Social Media: Emotion, Mediation, Anxiety and Contagion* (pp. 35–41). London: Rowman & Littlefield.

Tulloch, R. and Johnson, C. (2022). Games and Data Capture Culture: Play in the Era of Accelerated Neoliberalism. *Media, Culture & Society*, 44(5), 922–934.

van Dijck, J., Poell, T. and de Waal, M. (2018). *The Platform Society: Public Values in a Connective World*. Oxford: Oxford University Press.

Van Puyvelde, D. and Brantly, A. F. (2019). *Cybersecurity: Politics, Governance and Conflict in Cyberspace*. Cambridge: Polity.

Wilde, P. and Evans, A. (2019). Empathy at Play: Embodying Posthuman Subjectivities in Gaming. *Convergence*, 25(5–6), 791–806.

Winters, T. (2021). *The Metaverse: Prepare Now for the Next Big Thing!* Independently published.

Yar, M. and Steinmetz, K. F. (2019). *Cybercrime and Society* (3rd ed.). Los Angeles: SAGE.

Zickgraf, R. (2021, September 25). Mark Zuckerberg's "Metaverse" Is a Dystopian Nightmare. *Jacobin*, https://www.jacobinmag.com/2021/09/facebook-zuckerberg-metaverse-stephenson-big-tech.

6 Security, Regulation, and Other Challenges

In addition to offering multiple opportunities, the metaverse will also feature numerous threats and regulation challenges. To begin, the data necessitated by the metaverse will in itself be the source of threat, in ways that range from surveillance to hacking, also including malevolent sharing of data and the use of data for manipulation. Moreover, the metaverse will rekindle intellectual property (IP) debates, particularly with regard to the use of protected works, designs, and brands for user-generated content, counterfeit virtual goods, and unlicensed use or streaming of music or film. In addition, the metaverse would become a new domain and impetus for cyber-attacks and new forms of identity theft. Notably, ensuring security would become even more difficult owing to the diversity and complexity of the software and technology stack. Elsewhere, virtual harassment and assault would be a regular threat, but most legal systems are not necessarily prepared to treat such threats seriously enough. Related threats would involve new forms of defamation and revenge porn. Meanwhile, yet another set of questions regarding content pertain to ownership and whether platforms or their users should have property rights. The outcome of the latter debate would have significant consequences for both the security and economy of the metaverse. Finally, this chapter also addresses the status of NFTs and the associated financial risks. While some of such threats would be already recognisable security challenges taking on new forms ('old wine in new bottles'), others represent substantively new issues that can be only approximately mapped on to previous categories ('new wine in old bottles').

6.1 Old Wine in New Bottles

As the metaverse will, in all likelihood, span across most or all domains of life, a corollary is that 'any wrong that could be committed in the real world could also occur in the metaverse' (Abraham 2022). Crucially, though, there seems to still be very little oversight in this new domain, and, therefore,

DOI: 10.4324/9781003355861-6

everyone ends up being responsible for their own safety – or the safety of their possessions (see, generally, Mackenzie 2022). While at least some features of the metaverse, such as virtuality, interoperability, and its global nature, mean that some of the challenges and threats will be shared with the current internet, the significantly more intense level of datafication, the immersiveness of the experiences, and the new ways of living one's life and experiencing one's self virtually, among other things, will add a significant twist to already existing security issues.

As shown in this book, questions of governance and concentration of power – and, therefore, concentration of and control over data – will be among the central features of the development of the metaverse. However, it is already clear that huge amounts of data will be necessary to realistically render virtual worlds and experiences, including sensitive biometrical and behavioural data. Unavoidably, then, the breadth, level, and intensity of data collection in the metaverse would be 'unprecedented' as the very nature of the metaverse necessitates that platforms 'collect information about individuals' physiological responses, their movements and potentially even brainwave patterns, thereby gauging a much deeper understanding their customers' though process and behaviours' (Norton Rose Fulbright 2021; see also Lee 2022; Signé and Dooley 2022). This will unavoidably raise issues and concerns pertaining to privacy and user self-determination as the inferences made from such data can be used to nudge and manipulate users towards certain behaviours (purchase, voting, etc.) or used to make predictions on sensitive matters, such as health status (Mantegna 2021). In this sense, the user's avatar is not just (and, one might say, perhaps even not primarily) their digital representation but, instead, a proxy for datafication. After all, an avatar 'is your digital copy that lives based on your data', including biometric, browsing, and metaverse usage data (Ahvenainen 2022). Therefore, the avatar not only 'knows' one's personality to a highly intimate level – it also 'knows your health and physical condition' (Ahvenainen 2022). In fact, mass surveillance and data-based discrimination constitute a clear and imminent danger given the amount of data generated simply as a matter of accessing and acting in virtual settings and captured by the actors providing the hardware and the software that make the metaverse possible (Nwaneri 2017: 623). Similarly, Falchuk, Loeb and Neff (2018: 53) stress that '[t]he metaverse will surely be underpinned by data analytics software components and combined with big data analytics and machine learning'. For this reason, one of the key tasks for regulators will be to ensure that existing privacy laws apply to the metaverse at least as rigorously as they do to the current iteration of the internet. However, a renewed societal consensus regarding the status of data online is also necessary: while the current concern with privacy has given much impetus and legitimacy to the attempts by states and regional bodies to pass laws and regulations intended to protect user data, the same consensus for the metaverse should not be automatically assumed in advance; hence, an important role will also have to be played by civil society organisations to keep this matter on the agenda.

Moreover, the immersiveness of virtual environments also means that our behaviour is likely to be more authentic and reminiscent of our 'real-life' selves than e.g. simple browsing behaviour, which in turn means that the data collected is even more of a treasure trove (Henriksson 2018: 57–58). Crucially, since 'data is collected, shared, sold and inevitably hacked', there is a near-unavoidability that 'it will be weaponised by those seeking to profit or new ways to hurt or inundate – by ruthless advertisers, hateful trolls and malicious state actors' (Tremayne and Gill 2021). In addition, users should be worried not only about within-metaverse data that is being collected: as VR and, even more so, AR devices also need to constantly scan one's physical surroundings, that could also constitute a serious privacy risk (Braun 2019; Marr 2019). The extensiveness of data collection will also increase as users stay in the metaverse ever longer, being continuously monitored and thus enabling platforms and other data collectors 'to understand how best to service the users in an incredibly targeted way' (Norton Rose Fulbright 2021). Especially given the demographics of some of the current proto-metaverses (*Roblox* being the most prominent in this respect), children's data, which usually is also given special protection, will likely constitute a very large proportion of the data collected (Murphy et al. 2021). Under such circumstances, it is unsurprising that children's digital rights to privacy, play, and education have recently been explicitly brought under the remit of the UN Convention on the Rights of the Child (Livingstone 2021).

Notably, while, today, people have to turn on devices and open apps in order to be datafied, in the metaverse, user data 'will be gathered in the background while they go about their virtual lives' (Norton Rose Fulbright 2021). The global nature of the metaverse also means that significant attention will have to be paid to data protection across multiple jurisdictions, thus unavoidably creating a tension between data protection regimes and smooth operation of metaverse experiences. To add to the challenges, it is likely to be difficult to establish the exact responsibilities (including with regard to data protection) of actors behind the metaverse as this 'will likely involve picking apart a tangled web of relationships' between experience creators, platform providers, the companies underlying the metaverse as such, both as platforms and e.g. rendering engine providers, etc.; moreover, any such effort will likely only provide a few unequivocal answers owing to the overlap of functions and responsibilities (Murphy et al. 2021). In particular, the more integrated the metaverse becomes, the more challenges to privacy can be foreseen, particularly as a result of multiplication of data transfers, the necessity of new actors, such as data intermediaries necessary for any meaningful interoperability to take shape, and the spread and duplication of user data across multiple repositories with varying security standards (see e.g. Clifford Chance 2022).

Users will face other privacy threats as well. For example, the sharing of private information online with the intention to harass individuals – doxing – is not only on the rise globally but would also reach new levels of intrusiveness owing to the amount and sensitivity of data associated with the metaverse (Li and Lalani 2022). This may include, in addition to 'traditional' doxing, information such as virtual experiences and rooms visited (which might enable virtual stalking or reveal details of personal life that the individual would have preferred to keep to themselves) or body-to-avatar rendering data, which might enable sexual inferences or the creation of avatar clones, including non-consensual virtual sexbots. Next, as already stressed, disinformation and manipulation would reach another level in the metaverse by way of gaming users' information acquisition, designing experiences and games that push fake news on a visceral level, or abusing public rooms and spaces by converging large numbers of avatars (human and synthetic) for the purpose of indoctrination and radicalisation (Hinduja 2022; on the use of social bots, see also generally Hagen et al. 2022). Moreover, the immersiveness of the metaverse will make 'our current-day complications of out-of-context sound bites, trolling tweets, and faulty scientific claims feel quaint', and the more decentralisation there would be, the more difficult it would become to stop toxic content (Ball 2022: 291). Likewise, the capacity to tailor environments and experiences based on the ever-larger amounts of data available would only further increase the seriousness of the disinformation problem by simply making the content impossible for the user to ignore and not to believe in (Moynihan, Buchser and Wallace 2022).

Given the scope and diversity of data and privacy threats, it should come as no surprise that calls are already being made for governments to legislate on matters of content moderation, privacy protection (not just because of intrusive corporate practices but also because of excessive surveillance by law enforcement), as well as greater transparency in the operation of metaverse platforms (see e.g. Access Now 2021). Moreover, given the complexity and uncertainty that characterises the metaverse, some would even argue against state regulators allowing the full rollout of new technologies without first going through regulatory sandboxes (see e.g. Entsminger, Esposito and Tse 2022). Nevertheless, given the strong commercial impetus behind the metaverse and the multi-billion investments that have already been made, there will undoubtedly be a strong pressure against any delays or attempts at regulatory initiatives likely emphasising matters of technology dominance and potential revenue or, rather, alleged loss thereof (similar arguments have already been deployed in opposition to the EU's AI Act – see e.g. Mao 2021; McAfee 2021; Mueller 2021).

Of no lesser importance is the matter of identity. Some of the questions are ethical – e.g. whether a white man can be represented by an avatar of a black woman (see e.g. Ball 2022: 293) – while others relate to, for example, sexual consent and gender transparency of the person behind the avatar one is having virtual sex with. Likewise, the proliferation of AI-driven avatars and increasing opportunities to, for example, set one's avatar in autonomous mode e.g. to stand in for routine or uninteresting interactions (Campbell and Jovanović 2022) raise the issue of disclosure as well. Moreover, should such information be withheld, there would likely be a marketplace for third-party solutions that would e.g. purport to determine an identity probability score based on the data available; the availability of data to such third parties and the privacy risks inherent in their operation – as well as the broader balance of transparency versus privacy in avatar-based interactions – will undoubtedly constitute an important area of legal and ethical debate in the near future.

The metaverse will also rekindle intellectual property-related debates. Notably, the amount of user-generated content means that application of intellectual property laws will become more complex, with regard to both the collective nature of creative processes in the metaverse as well as the thorny issues of the use of third-party intellectual property by users and the movement of intellectual property with the user (e.g. skins, garments, and other avatar enhancements) between different metaverse worlds (Murphy et al. 2021). Indeed, it becomes clear that achieving an interoperable open metaverse will likely be problematic not only owing to the issues of business models and technological compatibility but also owing to IP matters, such as licensing (Palumbo 2021). Issues of note would include e.g. character likeness, particularly in metaverse experiences that aim to profit from the popularity of trending TV shows, games, or other proprietary content or feature concerts of fake music star avatars, unlicensed use of skins and digital items (or production of counterfeit ones) as well as the geographical and platform scope of licences (when skins are only licensed for a particular geographical area or a single platform but are exported elsewhere, perhaps under the pretext of interoperability), illegal streaming of films or music within games and experiences, etc. Infringements are also likely in user-generated content where e.g. protected works are reproduced in virtual experiences or perhaps even put for sale or trademarks are used to add realism to user-generated content (see e.g. Ara et al. 2022; Kumar 2022; Lee 2022; ReedSmith 2022). All of these issues represent concerns that are not particularly new with regard to online content. However, it is already clear that the metaverse, at the very least, will increase the diversity of ways IP infringements are manifested. Moreover, owing to the scope of the metaverse, monitoring for infringements would become increasingly complicated, potentially necessitating advanced AI tools and, therefore, additional resources (CMS n.d.).

Next to be considered are cybersecurity threats. Once again, these are, in many ways, simply new manifestations of already well-known security issues. For example, phishing attacks and online scams are already a feature in today's proto-metaverses, posing a threat to online identities and crypto assets (Collard 2022; see also Ongweso 2022; Javers et al. 2022). Likewise, malware directed against crypto wallets is being used to steal assets, while ransomware would become an even bigger threat, given the likely centrality of avatars and digital identities to users' lives: while, for many individuals, there is often limited sensitive or otherwise valuable data to be locked out of, the same cannot be said of one's virtual identity and digital possessions, thus likely increasing the ransom one would be prepared to pay (Collard 2022; Dwivedi 2022). Moreover, as the amount and value of data collected and stored by various parties increase by the very nature of the metaverse, so will the scope of data breaches (and, owing to the size of the incentive, potentially the frequency as well). Owing to the prominence of biometric data for realistic rendering of the metaverse, the potential harm caused by a breach would be greater as well, encompassing the most intimate aspects of a person's life. A more exotic-sounding metaverse cyber threat is the so-called 'human joystick attack', whereby the virtual environment is manipulated deliberately to cause physical movements that put the individual in harm's way (Casey, Baggili and Yarramreddy 2019). The security of headsets, haptics systems, and other devices used to access the metaverse would have to be considered as well (Collard 2022). Vulnerabilities in such devices could be used not only to syphon off data but also to manipulate the content being rendered to the user. Hence, such devices would need regular patches and security updates – much like other devices, from PCs to smartphones (see e.g. Dwivedi et al. 2022).

Moreover, the metaverse will enable new kinds of identity theft as virtual replicas can be created for impersonation purposes, building on the vast array of personal and biometric data available on and through the metaverse. The scope of metaverse activities (socialising, shopping, work, etc.) also means that the harm of such impersonation could be very significant (Braun 2019; Marr 2019). This also leaves open the question of personality and image rights: while previously those only applied to celebrities, now everyone is a potential target, and so expansion of legal protection would seem justifiable. Short of impersonation, one's own authentic avatar could be something that gets out of control: through hacking, credential theft, data poisoning, etc., it could just as well start doing things for someone else's benefit (Ahvenainen 2022).

Security threats would also likely be amplified through the integration of various technologies – partly owing to compatibility issues and partly because of different vulnerabilities being stacked upon one another (Wang et al. 2022). Ultimately, the complexity arising from different technologies and standards being piled together can in itself be seen as a security risk (Dwivedi 2022) while simultaneously leading to an entanglement of responsibilities without meaningful coordination (Murphy et al. 2021). Most likely, the complexity-equals-insecurity nexus would also apply to the inner workings of the metaverse: in particular, the more interoperable the metaverse would become, the more interoperable the threats would be as well, with overall security approximating that of the weakest link. Moreover, the underlying technologies and tools that are used by multiple companies would become the most prized targets as they would allow threat actors to strike across the metaverse – think of it as the metaverse equivalent to e.g. the SolarWinds hack. Hence, an interoperable metaverse, touted by enthusiasts, would certainly not be the most secure one. For this reason, it is important to achieve, through consumer pressure, industry standards, and external regulation, that the cybersecurity practices of the metaverse companies are robust (Signé and Dooley 2022).

6.2 New Wine in Old Bottles

In addition to the transformation of existing threats, new sets of concerns will become highly pressing as well, such as '[d]igital wellbeing and the effects of virtual embodiment representations' on oneself and on others (Mantegna 2021). Owing to the importance of the avatar to one's self-expression and identity, as already stressed in this book, harm suffered by the digital representation of oneself will likely have offline implications as well. Hence, trolls and cyber-bullies are set to become even more of a threat, and the onus is on the platforms to make sure that effective means for ensuring safe use of the metaverse are in place (Henriksson 2018: 58–59). Notably, 'people respond physiologically to an attack in virtual reality as if it were real' – and that is still the case even if the avatar is by no means representative of the physical person (Lemley and Volokh 2018: 1105; see also McEvoy 2019). Hence, violence against or sexual assault of an avatar needs to be considered seriously, particularly since, with the development and adoption of haptic technology, physical sensation will become involved as well (Li and Lalani 2022). Nevertheless, virtual harms are still typically treated as less 'real' – even though they should arguably be treated on par with offline ones (Lemley and Volokh 2018: 1109; Yar and Steinmetz 2019;

see also Heller 2020). After all, if the metaverse is to live up to its promise of immersiveness and the feeling of presence beyond that of Web 2.0, then it is only natural that the harm suffered would be greater as well (Hinduja 2022).

The issue is not hypothetical as the metaverse is already facing a harassment problem that may or may not include inappropriate non-consensual contact (Wakefield 2022; see also Goode 2021; Signé and Dooley 2022). There are technological solutions to prevent unwanted and unsolicited contact, such as creation of a security bubble around an avatar so that permission needs to be granted for every physical contact made (Tabahriti 2022) or introduction of a specific gesture or control to instantly remove unwanted users from one's vicinity (Heller 2020). However, such a security bubble would do little to prevent verbal abuse or intentional manipulation of the virtual environment with the aim of inflicting psychological harm (Wakefield 2022). Solutions to that exist as well – for example, garbling the voices of strangers (see e.g. Mlot 2022). Nevertheless, one could also argue that the more safety and avatar-distancing features are added, the more any metaverse experience becomes deprived of the social richness that characterises offline interactions, which often depend on chance encounters and interactions. That is, protection from toxic behaviours would ultimately come to harm metaverse socialisation while also further enclosing individuals within their social and informational bubbles through unprecedented abilities to pick and choose one's social interactions. Moreover, technological challenges can be foreseen to hinder the application of distancing because, as the usership of metaverse experiences grows, constantly measuring personal spaces and distances between avatars and maintaining databases of who is allowed to interact with whom and under what conditions would become extremely computationally intensive (Wakefield 2022).

New tools and regulations will have to be developed in order to deal with threats to avatars since the current ones offer very limited protection, if any at all, once again owing to the lingering belief in the lesser 'reality' of virtual incidents (McEvoy 2019; Heller 2020; Robertson 2022), even though some states (e.g. the UK) are making strides to deal with communication-based harassment and other offences, but not necessarily virtual sexual assault (see Zima 2022). Nevertheless, most countries still lack adequate laws to deal even with earlier-generation online threats, such as deepfake revenge porn, and so the lack of tools for dealing with virtual harassment and abuse directed against one's avatar would be even more glaring (Li and Lalani 2022). Ultimately, the debate as to whether groping and other forms of sexual assault are really the same thing if they are virtual misses the bigger picture of the pervasiveness of toxic behaviour regardless of the environment – and the real emotional harm suffered; moreover, as the very aim of virtual experiences is to trick users into feeling that they are actually inside the virtual environment and experiencing the simulation as part of the virtual world, such virtual toxic behaviours are made to feel more real by extension as well (Basu 2021).

Matters would become less complicated if legal personality would be extended to the avatar as part of the human person (Robertson 2022). The extension of personality rights to the avatar would also help answer other questions, such as liability for avatar defamation, impersonation, or other harm pertaining directly to the avatar (CMS n.d.). That extension, however, is difficult to expect in the short term at least, as a cultural shift would be necessary first. In the meantime, platform-internal terms of conduct have to be relied upon – as every user has to agree to such rules while creating an account, the platform company can suspend or terminate the offender's account for breaching the terms of contract (Ara et al. 2022). Nevertheless, this alone might not necessarily be a satisfactory remedy for users at the receiving end of virtual harassment and assault.

The metaverse would also likely extend, and create new forms of, revenge porn – powered by high-fidelity avatars (closely corresponding to the physical body of the represented human person), deepfakes, synthetic voice construction, motion capture, and other emerging virtual and physical technologies (Ball 2022: 292). For example, it would not be impossible to create a virtual sexbot in another person's likeness or to render an AI-powered nude version of a person's avatar in an adult-only metaverse experience. Both psychological and (given the primacy of the avatar in the metaverse) reputational harm caused by such actions would be very serious. Moreover, as many of the early adopters transpire to be children and teenagers, their mixing with adults in a relatively unsupervised environment means that not only are encounters with age-inappropriate content likely but also a hunting ground is opened up for sexual predators (Oremus 2022; see also Clayton and Dyer 2022; Crawford and Smith 2022). There is already evidence of children being lured into sexualised virtual activities on platforms such as *Roblox* – a development that is particularly alarming given the steady rise of self-generated child sexual content overall (Li and Lalani 2022). To exacerbate the problem, even if age restrictions are put in place, they can be bypassed by spoofing age verification or using a family member's account. Biometric verification, for example, using the VR device's movement capture and rendering functions to match the bodily characteristics of the user with those typical of a person who matches age restrictions would be a more reliable option, but it is bound to raise privacy and data protection issues and have discriminatory results for some users – it all boils down to the question of what count as 'typical' characteristics and which (ethnic, racial, etc.) groups they are derived from.

Of course, introduction of new regulations will likely give rise to slippery slope arguments, claiming that games and other virtual experiences are full of activities that, if performed in 'real' life, would be illegal, such as shooting people or speed driving to mention a few, which would ultimately end up being banned as well by increasingly draconian laws (McEvoy 2019). However, there are notable differences between e.g. shooting at non-player characters or even at another person's avatar (or being shot at yourself) when playing a shooting game – because the choice of such a game itself involves implicit or explicit consent that this might happen – and, by contrast, attacking somebody's avatar in a non-game situation. Here, the greater the interoperability, the more prominent the risks. Even in the absence of proper interoperability *across* platforms, the multiplicity of games, rooms, and experiences *within* a single platform means that, if one could carry, for example, a virtual designer handbag as part of avatar customisation from one experience to another, the same would likely also apply to e.g. carrying a shotgun from a virtual first-person shooter game into places such as a virtual shopping mall, classroom, or place of religious worship. Item filtering or policing of virtual behaviours could constitute important aspects of (self-)regulation. However, given the differences in, for example, gun control laws in the offline world, a consistent approach to such and similar matters is unlikely.

Another important threat lies in the very user-generated nature that is increasingly characteristic of today's proto-metaverses and will likely undergird a future metaverse proper. In fact, such user-generated nature of experience across many platforms may in itself be seen as a threat, at least under some circumstances (Oremus 2022). For example, the darker side of *Roblox* already 'includes strip clubs, sex parties and Nazi re-enactments' (Herrman and Browning 2021) or recreations of mass shootings and terrorist attacks (Li and Lalani 2022). In fact, fascist communities have found a fertile ground in the proto-metaverses of today, even despite virtual environments using not just human content moderators but also AI tools to police the experiences they host; nevertheless, the already vast and constantly growing breadth of such platforms means that detecting and removing objectionable content is extremely difficult (D'Anastasio 2021). Also, the extensive content moderation necessary to remove potentially harmful experiences, maintain community standards, etc. would involve companies behind the metaverse listening in to the ongoing conversations (Wakefield 2022). Even if that is not actual human moderators delving into ongoing interactions but AI tools scanning for potential triggers, this might still be considered overly intrusive, particularly given that the metaverse would be broader in scope (and, therefore, involve more aspects of life being datafied) than e.g. the social media platforms of today. All of this suggests that content moderation would likely be one of the most complicated issues in the metaverse (Winters 2021: 17).

There are even more questions raised by user-generated content, such as digital generative art and the various games and experiences that will populate the metaverse. For example, with the development of generative AI tools (such as Open AI's *DALL-E 2*), it is becoming increasingly easy to generate not only items approximating artistic creations (the 'art-ness' of generative art is beyond the scope of this book) and photo-realistic images but also content that could be seen as manipulative (e.g. to illustrate conspiracy theories). The same would apply to user-generated experiences created using in-platform build modes. In all likelihood, platforms would apply strategies reminiscent of today's social media, such as a combination of human reporting and AI-based automatic scanning. However, the questions as to who decides what content can be generated and posted and who decides what counts as such (and how the content in question is differentiated from e.g. irony and satire) can be easily foreseen, as are debates pertaining to gatekeeping of the public sphere. Likewise, the democratisation of creativity that such pre-built tools enable will significantly increase the amount of questionable content, either from a security or from an IP point of view.

A further matter to consider is the ownership of items inside virtual platforms (both items created by users themselves and those made available to them as virtual purchases), that is, whether the platform owns everything, merely licensing (or sub-licensing) the use of content to its users, or allows direct item ownership by the users – a matter that is currently left for the platform owners to decide, with both approaches seeming equally tenable, at least for the time being (Zhou, Leenders and Cong 2018). One takeaway is clear: platforms *are* going to play a much more significant role in defining virtual property and the entitlements to the rights to such property as users are dependent on them for both creation/acquisition and possession of the items in question (Zhou, Leenders and Cong 2018). This dependence extends much further than e.g. state influence on the possession of physical property could extend. After all, states do not have control over the laws of nature that underlie the creation and existence of tangible objects and assets, whereas platform owners have full control of digital 'nature'. While, for example, Ahvenainen (2022) claims that, over time, digital ownership rights will become identical to offline property rights, this overlooks some important differences, including the move towards the 'as-a-service' model discussed previously in the book, the wholly platform-contingent nature of existence of both the avatar and virtual items, etc. (for more on the differences and transformations of ownership, see e.g. Perzanowski and Schultz 2016). After all, even offline, the very notion and characteristics of private property have undergone major changes and are completely contingent upon past political, cultural, and philosophical struggles (see e.g. von Benda-Beckmann, von Benda Beckmann and Wiber 2009; Huffman 2013; Kanatli 2022).

The platform ownership scenario would be significantly less conducive to a virtual economy with individuals unable to trade and otherwise monetise that which they do not fully own. On the other hand, this would be a more secure scenario in the sense of all assets being affixed to the corresponding users in a centralised database, at least absent a platform-wide hack. While some instances of illegal copying and use may appear, they would likely be suboptimal from a quality and ease-of-use perspective and, therefore, rare (a metaverse equivalent of print-screening content that cannot be straightforwardly saved). Meanwhile, in the case where private ownership becomes the norm, a secondary market for digital goods and assets would be opened up, stimulating a virtual economy but simultaneously opening up a list of threats, including, but not limited to, fraud (misrepresenting the goods and assets to be sold or acquisition of legitimate assets through deceit), phishing and hacking (gaining access to an individual's account to steal assets), or perhaps deletion (destruction) of the assets altogether. Moreover, virtual assets could be used for money laundering (see e.g. Schwartz et al. 2021).

A further matter of ownership is that of the avatar itself. This encompasses the avatar as such, its appearance, the code behind it, its associated data, and its 'belongings' (skins, accessories, etc.); likewise, a question might be raised as to who has the right to make changes to the avatar (e.g. through updates to the underlying code) and even terminate it (Ahvenainen 2022). A further extension of the question also concerns the status of the victim should a crime be committed against an avatar: whether the person represented by that avatar is the victim (even if they do not have full property rights over the avatar) or the platform (if it owns the avatar), or, perhaps, both. Moreover, if individual property rights end up being a metaverse standard, it is not clear what happens if a new update issued by a platform renders certain assets no longer compatible with their section of the metaverse or with the way avatars are subsequently rendered. While users would probably expect to be compensated for their inability to enjoy their property (which could have been expensive), such an outcome would hardly be possible – after all, particularly with regard to third-party content, it would be disproportionate for a company to keep track of all possible formats and add-ons, thereby leaving users at risk when it comes to the stability of their virtual possessions.

In all likelihood, there would be a difficult-to-disentangle mixture of personal and platform ownership (particularly should there be some level of interoperability, so that users would have acquired assets on different platforms with different ownership policies) as well as property rights of those who have licensed certain elements (skins, for example) to a particular platform. Potential challenges abound here, particularly because, as already established in this book, an avatar, with its associated virtual assets, goes beyond the status of a simple digital stand-in but is coextensive with the actual person behind it. Simultaneously, though, as with ownership more generally, a platform-centric model of avatar ownership would help preclude certain illicit activities ranging from the use of counterfeit skins to some forms of avatar misuse (since onus would be on the platform as the owner to validate transactions and to take all necessary measures to ensure that only legitimate users have access to accounts). Likewise, platform ownership would help ensure that bot and zombie accounts (the latter referring to abandoned accounts or those indefinitely left on automated mode) would be kept to a minimum. On the other hand, as is typically the case, greater security comes with a trade-off – in this case, an almost unchecked power of platform companies over virtual life. Therefore, platform abuse of power would likely constitute no lesser a threat to users than hostile actors in the more decentralised scenario.

In addition, there would likely be a necessity to regulate AI agents owing to their manipulative potential (Rosenberg 2022). In some cases, these could act as avatar-embodied virtual assistants, for example, nudging their user's attention towards sponsored content (Rosenberg 2022). Such virtual assistants (or virtual slaves, as per previous chapter) could be either malicious by design (particularly if they are to be purchased from third-party vendors – just as today one can download malware posing as legitimate software) or made malicious through hacking or data poisoning, or they might simply have predesigned back doors for sponsored content masquerading as advice. Owing to reliance on such assistants, a user would be manipulated into making personal, political, economic, etc. choices that are not for their own benefit but, instead, follow the interests of other parties. Another potential scenario could be the use of automated avatars for catfishing (the use of a fictitious persona to trick somebody into a relationship, often for financial gain – see e.g. Hinduja 2022). Particularly with the use of behavioural and data analysis in order to better understand and predict the behaviours and emotions of the targeted users, the effectiveness of such practices could be alarmingly high. In other cases, though, such automated agents could act as disseminators of propaganda and hate. Who is responsible for avatar behaviour and who has the duty to preclude them from engaging in harmful behaviour (the creator, the operator, the platform, etc.), as well as what is to be done when such agents have autonomous learning capacity (and, therefore, who is liable when harm is suffered), are questions that will necessitate regulatory responses.

There are also important regulatory matters pertaining to NFTs and tokens, particularly where NFTs can be treated as securities or are advertised as investment opportunities; in some cases, it might be difficult to even differentiate between utility and security tokens (Ara et al. 2022; Clifford Chance 2022; ReedSmith 2022; Bundi and Bourgaux n.d.) as in, for example, Bored Ape Yacht Club NFTs that act simultaneously as quasi-investment opportunities and access keys to virtual content, including a dedicated metaverse experience. However, the investment aspect of NFTs might entail significant financial risk to the consumers who would be left unprotected by traditional schemes. Same considerations might also apply to decentralised apps that rely on tokens that promise either fractionalisation of ownership or entitlement to a potential revenue stream should the app take off, although further clarifications from regulatory authorities would be necessary (Ara et al. 2022; ReedSmith 2022). Extending the laws governing securities and investment to such tokens would be a welcome development as that would introduce control and regulation to the issuance of tokens and provide extra protection to individuals who are currently left to bear the risks. However, the issues of jurisdiction and enforcement would have to be somehow resolved.

While this overview of challenges and threats likely to be caused by the metaverse is not exhaustive, and the practical implementation of this environment will undoubtedly bring about as yet unforeseen issues to the fore, it nevertheless points out the main directions in which law and industry self-regulation are likely to tread. As the metaverse is going to take up an ever-larger part of everyday life, such considerations will only become ever more pertinent. For this reason, it is crucial that lawyers, politicians, and technology insiders work together to ensure maximisation of the benefits and minimisation of the risks of this emerging new environment.

Bibliography

Abraham, A. (2022, April 4). Law & Order in the Metaverse. *FinExtra*, https://www.finextra.com/the-long-read/376/law--order-in-the-metaverse.

Access Now. (2021, December 9). Virtual Worlds, Real People: Human Rights in the Metaverse, https://www.accessnow.org/human-rights-metaverse-virtual-augmented-reality/.

Ahvenainen, J. (2022, January 28). Metaverses Are Coming, but Who Owns Your Avatar? *Medium*, https://medium.com/prifina/metaverses-are-coming-but-who-owns-your-avatar-61ae9750f9c2.

Ara, T. K. et al. (2022, June 22). Exploring the Metaverse: What Laws Will Apply? *DLA Piper*, https://www.dlapiper.com/en/france/insights/publications/2022/06/exploring-the-metaverse-ipt-news-june-2022/.

Ball, M. (2022). *The Metaverse and How It will Revolutionize Everything*. New York: Liveright Publishing Corporation.

Basu, T. (2021, December 16). The Metaverse Has a Groping Problem Already. *MIT Technology Review*, https://www.technologyreview.com/2021/12/16/1042516/the-metaverse-has-a-groping-problem/.

Braun, A. (2019, February 14). Security, Privacy, Virtual Reality: How Hacking Might Affect VR and AR. *IoT Tech Trends*, https://www.iottechtrends.com/how-hacking-affect-vr-ar/.

Bundi, D. and Bourgaux, V. (n.d.). Legal & Compliance in the Metaverse. *PwC Switzerland*, https://www.pwc.ch/en/insights/regulation/legal-compliance-metaverse.html.

Campbell, M. and Jovanović, M. (2022). Digital Self: The Next Evolution of the Digital Human. *IEEE Computer*, 55, 82–86.

Casey, P., Baggili, I. and Yarramreddy, A. (2019). Immersive Virtual Reality Attacks and the Human Joystick. *IEEE Transactions on Dependable and Secure Computing*, 18(2), 550–562.

Clayton, J. and Dyer, J. (2022, February 15). Roblox: The Children's Game with a Sex Problem. *BBC*, https://www.bbc.com/news/technology-60314572.

Clifford Chance. (2022, February). The Metaverse: What Are the Legal Implications? https://www.cliffordchance.com/content/dam/cliffordchance/briefings/2022/02/the-metaverse-what-are-the-legal-implications.pdf.

CMS. (n.d.). Trademarks and Copyright, NFTs and Civil Law Principles in the Metaverse, https://cms.law/en/int/publication/legal-issues-in-the-metaverse/part-2-trademarks-and-copyright-nfts-and-civil-law-principles-in-the-metaverse.

Collard, A. (2022, August 18). Crime in the Metaverse Is Very Real: But How Do We Police a World With no Borders or Bodies? *World Economic Forum*, https://www.weforum.org/agenda/2022/08/crime-punishment-metaverse/.

Crawford, A. and Smith, T. (2022, February 23). Metaverse App Allows Kids into Virtual Strip Clubs. *BBC*, https://www.bbc.com/news/technology-60415317.

D'Anastasio, C. (2021, June 10). How *Roblox* Became a Playground for Virtual Fascists. *Wired*, https://www.wired.com/story/roblox-online-games-irl-fascism-roman-empire/.

Dwivedi, Y. K., Hughes, L., Baabdullah, A. M., Ribeiro-Navarrete, S., Giannakis, M., Al-Debei, M. M. Dennehy, D., Metri, B., Buhalis, D., Cheung, C. M. K., Conboy, K., Doyle, R., Dubey, R., Dutot, V., Felix, R., Goyal, D. P., Gustafsson A., Hinsch, C. Jebabli, I., Janssen, M., Wamba, S. F. (2022). Metaverse Beyond the Hype: Multidisciplinary Perspectives on Emerging Challenges, Opportunities, and Agenda for Research, Practice and Policy. *International Journal of Information Management*, 66, 1–55.

Entsminger, J., Esposito, M. and Tse, T. (2022, August 17). Who Will Establish Metaverse Ethics? *Project Syndicate*, https://www.project-syndicate.org/commentary/who-establishes-metaverse-ethics-by-josh-entsminger-et-al-2022-08.

Falchuk, B., Loeb, S. and Neff, R. (2018). The Social Metaverse: Battle for Privacy. *IEEE Technology and Society Magazine*, 37(2), 52–61.

Goode, L. (2021, August 27). The Architects of the Metaverse Need to Read the Virtual Room. *Wired*, https://www.wired.com/story/plaintext-architects-metaverse-diversity/.

Hagen, L., Neely, S., Keller, T. E., Scharf, R. and Vasquez, F. E. (2022). Rise of the Machines? Examining the Influence of Social Bots on a Political Discussion Network. *Social Science Computer Review*, 40(2), 264–287.

Heller, B. (2020). Reimagining Reality: Human Rights and Immersive Technology. *Harvard Kennedy School Carr Center for Human Rights Policy Discussion Paper*, https://carrcenter.hks.harvard.edu/files/cchr/files/ccdp_2020-008_brittanheller.pdf.

Henriksson, E. A. (2018). Data Protection Challenges for Virtual Reality Applications. *Interactive Entertainment Law Review*, 1(1), 57–61.

Herrman, J. and Browning, K. (2021, July 10). Are We in the Metaverse Yet? *The New York Times*, https://www.nytimes.com/2021/07/10/style/metaverse-virtual-worlds.html.

Hinduja, S. (2022, May 11). The Metaverse: Opportunities, Risks, and Harms. *Cyberbullying Research Center*, https://cyberbullying.org/metaverse.

Huffman, J. L. (2013). *Private Property and State Power: Philosophical Justifications, Economic Explanations, and the Role of Government*. London: Palgrave Macmillan.

Javers, E. et al. (2022, May 26). Cybercriminals Target Metaverse Investors with Phishing Scams. *CNBC*, https://www.cnbc.com/2022/05/26/cybercriminals-target-metaverse-investors-with-phishing-scams.html.

Kanatli, M. (2022). *Private Property, Freedom and Order: Social Contract Theories from Hobbes to Rawls*. London: Routledge.

Kumar, N. (2022, February 17). Six Unaddressed Legal Concerns for the Metaverse. *Forbes*, https://www.forbes.com/sites/forbestechcouncil/2022/02/17/six-unaddressed-legal-concerns-for-the-metaverse/?sh=2479b7927a94.

Lee, Y.-H. (2022, May 27). The Legal Wild West of the Metaverse – Its Legal Implications. *JDSupra*, https://www.jdsupra.com/legalnews/the-legal-wild-west-of-the-metaverse-4470767/.

Lemley, M. A. and Volokh, E. (2018). Virtual Reality and Augmented Reality. *University of Pennsylvania Law Review*, 66(5), 1051–1138.

Li, C. and Lalani, F. (2022, January 14). How to Address Digital Safety in the Metaverse. *World Economic Forum*, https://www.weforum.org/agenda/2022/01/metaverse-risks-challenges-digital-safety/.

Livingstone, S. (2021, March 24). Children's Rights Apply in the Digital World! *LSE*, https://blogs.lse.ac.uk/parenting4digitalfuture/2021/03/24/general-comment-25/.

Mackenzie, S. (2022). Criminology Towards the Metaverse: Cryptocurrency Scams, Grey Economy and the Technosocial. *The British Journal of Criminology*, doi: 10.1093/bjc/azab118.

Mantegna, M. (2021, June 10). The Metaverse: A Brave, New (Virtual) World. *Medium*, https://medium.com/berkman-klein-center/the-metaverse-a-brave-new-virtual-world-2f040cbae7d4.

Mao, Y. M. (2021, July 28). The EU's Artificial Intelligence Act Could Become a Brake on Innovation. *Finextra*, https://www.finextra.com/blogposting/20685/the-eus-artificial-intelligence-act-could-become-a-brake-on-innovation.

Marr, B. (2019, July 17). The Important Risks and Dangers of Augmented and Virtual Reality. *Forbes*, https://www.forbes.com/sites/bernardmarr/2019/07/17/the-important-risks-and-dangers-of-virtual-and-augmented-reality/?sh=24bc1843d50e.

McAfee, A. (2021, July 25). EU Proposals to Regulate AI Are Only Going to Hinder Innovation. *Financial Times*, https://www.ft.com/content/a5970b6c-e731-45a7-b75b-721e90e32e1c.

McEvoy, F. J. (2019, December 9). If Virtual Reality is Reality, Virtual Abuse is Just Abuse. *Towards Data Science*, https://towardsdatascience.com/if-virtual-reality-is-reality-virtual-abuse-is-just-abuse-34f09f1007ef.

Mlot, S. (2022, June 14). Meta Is Adding a Garbled Voice Option for Strangers in Horizon Worlds. *PCMag*, https://www.pcmag.com/news/meta-is-adding-a-garbled-voice-option-for-strangers-in-horizon-worlds.

Moynihan, H., Buchser, M. and Wallace, J. (2022, April 25). What is the Metaverse? *Chatham House*, https://www.chathamhouse.org/2022/04/what-metaverse.

Mueller, B. (2021, July 26). How Much will the Artificial Intelligence Act Cost Europe? *Information Technology & Innovation Foundation*, https://itif.org/publications/2021/07/26/how-much-will-artificial-intelligence-act-cost-europe/.

Murphy, S. et al. (2021, July). The Metaverse: The Evolution of a Universal Digital Platform. *Norton Rose Fulbright*, https://www.nortonrosefulbright.com/en-us/knowledge/publications/5cd471a1/the-metaverse-the-evolution-of-a-universal-digital-platform.

Norton Rose Fulbright. (2021, July). The Metaverse: The Evolution of a Universal Digital Platform, https://www.nortonrosefulbright.com/en/knowledge/publications/5cd471a1/the-metaverse-the-evolution-of-a-universal-digital-platform.

Nwaneri, C. (2017). Ready Lawyer One: Legal Issues in the Innovation of Virtual Reality. *Harvard Journal of Law & Technology*, 30(2), 601–627.

Ongweso, E. (2022, May 3). Scammers Net $5M In Stolen NFTs After BAYC Virtual Land Sale Disaster. *Vice*, https://www.vice.com/en/article/n7nxw8/scammers-net-dollar5m-in-stolen-nfts-after-bayc-virtual-land-sale-disaster.

Oremus, W. (2022, February 7). Kids Are Flocking to Facebook's 'Metaverse'. Experts Worry Predators Will Follow. *The Washington Post*, https://www.washingtonpost.com/technology/2022/02/07/facebook-metaverse-horizon-worlds-kids-safety/.

Palumbo, J. (2021, December 21). Digital Dress Codes: What Will We Wear in the Metaverse? *CNN*, https://edition.cnn.com/style/article/metaverse-digital-fashion/index.html.

Perzanowski, A. and Schultz, J. (2016). *The End of Ownership: Personal Property and the Digital Economy*. Cambridge: The MIT Press.

ReedSmith. (2022, August). *Reed Smith Guide to the Metaverse* (2nd ed.), https://www.reedsmith.com/-/media/files/metaverse/guidetothemetaverse2ndedition.pdf.

Robertson, A. (2022, February 4). Meta Is Adding a 'Personal Boundary' to VR Avatars to Tackle Harassment. *The Verge*, https://www.theverge.com/2022/2/4/22917722/meta-horizon-worlds-venues-metaverse-harassment-groping-personal-boundary-feature.

Rosenberg, L. (2022, January 27). The Danger of AI Micro-Targeting in the Metaverse. *Venture Beat*, https://venturebeat.com/2022/01/27/the-danger-of-ai-micro-targeting-in-the-metaverse/.

Schwarz, N. et al. (2021). Virtual Assets and Anti-Money Laundering and Combating the Financing of Terrorism: Some Legal and Practical Considerations. *International Monetary Fund*, https://www.imf.org/en/Publications/fintech-notes/Issues/2021/10/14/Virtual-Assets-and-Anti-Money-Laundering-and-Combating-the-Financing-of-Terrorism-1-463654.

Signé, L. and Dooley, H. (2022, July 21). A Proactive Approach Toward Addressing the Challenges of the Metaverse. *The Bookings Institution*, https://www.brookings.edu/techstream/a-proactive-approach-toward-addressing-the-challenges-of-the-metaverse/.

Tabahriti, S. (2022, February 5). Meta Is Putting a Stop to Virtual Groping in Its Metaverse by Creating 4-Foot Safety Bubbles Around Avatars. *Business Insider*, https://www.businessinsider.com/meta-metaverse-virtual-groping-personal-boundary-safety-bubble-horizons-venues-2022-2.

Tremayne, T. and Gill, R. (2021, July 7). We Need to Kick Big Tech Out of the Metaverse. *Wired*, https://www.wired.co.uk/article/metaverse-big-tech.

von Benda-Beckmann, F., von Benda-Beckmann, K. and Wiber, M. G. (2009). The Properties of Property. In F. von Benda-Beckmann, K. von Benda-Beckmann and M. G. Wiber (eds.) *Changing Properties of Property* (pp. 1–39). New York: Berghahn Books.

Wakefield, J. (2022, February 4). Meta Moves to Tackle Creepy Behaviour in Virtual Reality. *BBC*, https://www.bbc.com/news/technology-60247542.

Wang, Y. et al. (2022). A Survey on Metaverse: Fundamentals, Security, and Privacy. *Arxiv*, https://arxiv.org/pdf/2203.02662.pdf.

Winters, T. (2021). *The Metaverse: Prepare Now for the Next Big Thing!* Independently published.

Yar, M. and Steinmetz, K. F. (2019). *Cybercrime and Society* (3rd ed.). Los Angeles: SAGE.

Zhou, M., Leenders, M. A. A. M. and Cong, L. M. (2018). Ownership in the Virtual World and the Implications for Long-Term User Innovation Success. *Technovation*, 78, 56–65.

Zima, M. (2022, June 7). The Metaverse: Virtual Offences, Real World Penalties? *Solicitors Journal*, https://www.solicitorsjournal.com/sjarticle/the-metaverse-avatars-and-sex-law/605537.

7 Concluding Thoughts

According to the more enthusiastic voices, the metaverse, combining the features of content streaming, gaming, social media, e-commerce, and any other conceivable domain, should also have the combined appeal of them all (see e.g. Hackl, Lueth and Di Bartolo 2022: 92). While such arguments appear to be rather simplistic, it is nevertheless likely that the metaverse will become the new normal, although more likely through a combination of genuine appeal and network effects. Of course, instead of coming about through a single magical leap, 'the Metaverse will be produced through the partial integration of many competing virtual world platforms and technologies' (Ball 2022: 63). That, however, might become a societal and political problem: absent a clear shock of radical change, any negative undersides to the metaverse would materialise as gradual encroachments on preferable ways of life and thus largely avoid scrutiny.

It is crucial to note that the metaverse will be an automatically rendered immersive and adaptive world where, while humans would perhaps still need to do the thinking, the surroundings adapt seamlessly, and new experiences can be constructed from scratch (think of something akin to *GPT-3* or *DALL-E 2* tailored for the whole of one's surroundings). This would have further cultural significance as automated content generation is only going to increase the dominance of the largest cultures and languages, simply because there is more data to support content generation; that is, unless communities take matters into their own hands and establish their own datafication-generation initiatives (Hao 2022). In this way, the metaverse would bring about if not ever-deeper homogenisation of global culture then at least homogenisation around global cultural clusters (as a result of both regulatory splintering and identity politics), each centred around a cultural behemoth and becoming an intense projection of soft power.

There are legitimate concerns about the escapism offered by the metaverse distracting humans from serious offline problems by prioritising virtual fantasies. Likewise, Bailenson (2018: 250) predicts that virtual

DOI: 10.4324/9781003355861-7

experiences may well be addictive: after all, why one would go for anything else 'if the best experiences imaginable can be had at the press of a button'? In a similar manner, for Gault (2021), 'the goal is to achieve a fantasy world better and more fascinating than the real one'. The metaverse thus becomes a fantasy world in the broadest sense – for example, Terry and Keeney (2022: 6) describe personal user spaces in the metaverse in terms of enabling otherwise unaffordable experiences ('a corner office overlooking Central Park') or pure fantasy spaces and combining them with apps and productivity tools, including a personal AI workforce to help carry out tasks. Hence, the metaverse is seen as democratising the double fantasy of success and achievement. Likewise, Greengard (2019: 181) emphasises the feelings of withdrawal and sadness after 'returning' from virtual experiences and finding physical reality to be less exciting than the digital fantasy; to that effect, prolonged immersion in virtual experiences can reduce the sense of presence and stake in physical reality. Similarly, the aspect of instant gratification is also stressed by Stiegler (2021: 5), for whom virtual experiences constitute 'a world in which all it takes is to put on a headset and it is all there: friends, family, shopping, news, education, love, and sex'. Indeed, the offline world cannot compete.

Moreover, such experiences would not simply be there – they would also be immersive and, therefore, in a way 'real'. Effectively, the very notion of 'reality' would then likely stop making clear sense, necessitating a rethink of some of the most fundamental ontological distinctions and of the ways in which the natural and the social worlds are experienced (Lemley and Volokh 2018: 1056; Greengard 2019: 211). The perceived merger of (or, at the very least, indifference to) the virtual and the physical would then be the logical next step (Greengard 2019: 209; see also Rubin 2020: 124; Hackl, Lueth and Di Bartolo 2022: 202). Hence, for example, an avatar and a person, as well as the actions they perform, would be equally 'real'. The above clearly suggests a need to move towards 'a more-than-human consideration' of how the human body, by way of 'sensory perceptions, thoughts, memories, desires, imaginings, physical movements and feelings', becomes inseparable from technologies (Lupton 2020: 18). Ultimately, reality would become akin to a set of building blocks without building instructions, leaving room for everyone to arrange those blocks in their own personalised fashion (Rubin 2020: 231–232). Nevertheless, it is also clear that the available selection, shapes, and sizes of such blocks would still directly impact what can be built. For that reason, competition over determining the set of blocks will be strong (for a similar argument, see e.g. Ball 2022: 17).

Still, it is often the case that accounts of the metaverse also borrow an important discursive construction from the current debates on the Internet of Things, AI, and other digital technologies by assuming 'a seamless deployment and public acceptance' while strategically ignoring 'the mundane, messy, frustrating, and sometimes frightening and dangerous realities of living with these technologies' (Lupton 2020). To this effect, as Nowotny (2022: 93) argues, technological progress becomes discursively linked with human and societal progress so that the more leeway is given to the former, the more, correspondingly, there is proclaimed to be of the latter. Consequently, a common strategy employed by metaverse enthusiasts involves creating a sense of urgency, great opportunities about to be missed, or race to remain relevant (see, characteristically, Hackl and Buzzell 2021: 201–202; Hackl, Lueth and Di Bartolo 2022: 68). The problem with this rush, however, is that implementation standards can easily become a race to the lowest common denominator owing to adopters rushing on without properly understanding the nature and effects of the new domain.

Bibliography

Bailenson, J. (2018). *Experience on Demand: What Virtual Reality Is, How It Works, and What It Can Do*. New York: W. W. Norton & Company.

Ball, M. (2022). *The Metaverse and How It Will Revolutionize Everything*. New York: W. W. Norton & Company.

Gault, M. (2021, February 15). Billionaires See VR as a Way to Avoid Radical Social Change. *Wired*, https://www.wired.com/story/billionaires-use-vr-avoid-social-change/.

Greengard, S. (2019). *Virtual Reality*. Cambridge: The MIT Press.

Hackl, C. and Buzzell, J. (2021). *The Augmented Workforce* (2nd ed.). North Kansas City: Renown Publishing.

Hackl, C., Lueth, D. and Di Bartolo, T. (2022). *Navigating the Metaverse: A Guide to Limitless Possibilities in a Web 3.0 World*. Hoboken: Wiley.

Hao, K. (2022, April 22). A New Vision of Artificial Intelligence for the People. *MIT Technology Review*, https://www.technologyreview.com/2022/04/22/1050394/artificial-intelligence-for-the-people/.

Lemley, M. A. and Volokh, E. (2018). Virtual Reality and Augmented Reality. *University of Pennsylvania Law Review*, 66(5), 1051–1138.

Lupton, D. (2020). *Data Selves*. Cambridge: Polity.

Nowotny, H. (2022). *In AI We Trust: Power, Illusion and Control of Predictive Algorithms*. Cambridge: Polity.

Rubin, P. (2020). *Future Presence: How Virtual Reality is Changing Human Connection, Intimacy, and the Limits of Ordinary Life*. New York: Harper One.

Stiegler, C. (2021). *The 360° Gaze: Immersions in Media, Society, and Culture*. Cambridge: The MIT Press.

Terry, Q. and Keeney, S. (2022). *The Metaverse Handbook: Innovating for the Internet's Next Tectonic Shift*. Hoboken: Wiley.

Index